The Golden Age British Truckin

D1147740

Time was when the image of a lorry didn't sum up the much maligned and often unjustified image of a huge juggernaut thundering along motorways or through the narrow streets of small villages; or inches from your Mini's rear bumper.

Instead, this book takes you back into another world. To the days when lorries were much smaller, often had lots of curves and, in many cases, a big chrome radiator grille. They were almost without doubt built in Britain, which had dozens of manufacturers, sporting names which just conjured up heavy engineering and solidity: Scammell, Seddon, Foden, and even Vulcan.

No-one would suggest for a moment these great makes of yesteryear had the creature comforts of today's vehicles. Heaters were a luxury until the turn of the sixties, for example; drivers have told tales of their boots freezing to the floor in the worst conditions... while they were driving! In winter there was always the danger of being stuck in snow… without a mobile phone to summon assistance. Cabs would often be sweltering hot in summer, and noisy and uncomfortable at all times. Power steering and automatic gearboxes? Forget it!

No warm and cosy sleeping area to bed down in and watch a film on DVD at night. Instead drivers would stay in digs, many of which were real homes from home, but some were err… not.

Meals would be eaten in one of the many transport cafes throughout the land, following a trudge through murky puddles in the parking area outside. Again, standards could vary but there were many excellent and today much-missed legendary establishments, like the Jungle Café at Shap in Cumberland.

Motorways were non-existent and ring roads thin on the ground, so lorries would have to drive through the centre of towns and cities. For many years, vehicles had a legal top speed of 20mph, which didn't tend to get drivers home too early.

Lorry drivers still took a deep pride in their job and often kept their vehicles immaculate. They had a camaraderie largely missing today. The lack of tachographs and mobile phones meant much more freedom on the open road, though some men were forced to work incredibly long hours.

Haulage companies were also relatively free of today's red tape, but there was a complex licensing system governing which goods could be carried, and in which areas.

Along with small family-owned hauliers there were many major firms, again most long gone. The post-war Labour Government

nationalised much of the industry into British Road Services but the following Conservative administration reversed this process.

Many firms were virtually household names, such as Carter Paterson, whereas others were renowned within the industry, great names such as Fisher Renwick, Crow Carrying Co and Hay's Wharf.

All this sums up a lost world, but thanks to the efforts of so many lorry preservationists we have a superb representative selection of these vehicles from the past. Many have been built from piles of rusty metal into beautiful show winning vehicles bristling with character. Some have been restored on large budgets, others not.

They include lorries ranging from those built before the First World War to those dating from the 1980s. Now, earlier Volvos and Scanias, along with other Continental makes are just as cherished as their British equivalents – and rightly so.

This book looks at everything, from restorations to family histories and we go back through photographs to many times past.

We've lorries which delivered goods once known to everyone (remember Benson's Toffees and Mother's Pride bread) and many other matters to jog your memory.

Have a great read, marvel at the skills of vehicles and most importantly, drink deeply from this overflowing cup of nostalgia!

Nick Larkin,
Editor, Classic & Vintage Commercials

Printed by: William Gibbons Ltd.
Tel: +44 (0) 1902 730011   www.williamgibbons.co.uk

On behalf of
Kelsey Publishing Group, Cudham Tithe Barn, Berrys Hill, Cudham, Kent. TN16 3AG. ENGLAND.
Tel: +44 (0) 1959 541444   Fax: +44 (0) 1959 541400   www.kelsey.co.uk
First edition 2006© Second edition 2007© ISBN number: 978187309881-3

KELSEY PUBLISHING GROUP

CLASSIC & Vintage COMMERCIALS

Contents...

CONFESSIONS OF A TRUCK PHOTOGRAPHER

Peter Davies looks back on half a century of photographing lorries and ponders why the subject fascinates him so much.

Below: One of my earliest pictures shows a new Thornycroft tipper, registered EEJ 397. The vehicle, which I think is a Sturdy, is seen crossing Trecefel railway bridge on the outskirts of Tregaron, Cardiganshire. It is in the cream and black livery of local builders' merchants J D Lloyd and Sons, and was photographed on my brother's Paxina 29 camera on October 3, 1955.

Also taken in 1955 is this hasty shot of a 1946 AEC Monarch registered KPC 854. The 1500-gallon milk tanker operated out of the local Milk Marketing Board creamery at Pont Llanio and, at that time, was making regular trips to Conway's Dairies in Merthyr Tydfil. MMB vehicles were registered in Surrey, where the board had its headquarters at Thames Ditton.

People often ask me why I take photographs of trucks, or lorries as I still prefer to call them. Well, there's no simple answer to that. Why would people take photographs of wildlife, scenery or architecture? Perhaps the answer is to place on record something that interests them, something they have pleasure in seeing again and again. Alternatively, it might be argued that some photographers' motives can be purely mercenary.

After half a century during which l have taken well over 100,000 lorry photos, I still can't give a straight answer. My lorry photography was certainly not born of an interest in photography - that was just a means to an end.

For as long as I can remember I have had an all-consuming interest in lorries. Even at primary school I used to draw pictures of lorries in my exercise books. So it seemed a good idea to also take photos of lorries when the opportunity arose.

Of course there were obstacles in the way of my plans - like, for instance, not owning a camera! I was forced to beg the loan of a camera from my elder brother, a Paxina 29 6x6cm or sometimes from my father, who owned a tatty folding Kodak dating from the 1920s.

Both cameras, though quite different in design, presented problems, especially in focusing. Neither had a rangefinder, so it was a case of guesswork. I lost count of the number of pictures I ruined through not engaging the lens in the right position.

The old Kodak was particularly unpredictable, as the viewfinder was tiny and the image was viewed through a sort of pea soup. Coupled with this there was a small pinhole in the bellows. This often let light in, creating dark streaks over the negative, ruining an otherwise nice picture.

As my pocket money was pegged at 2.5 new pence a week in the mid-1950s it took a while to save up for a film, not to mention the cost of developing and printing. Consequently not many pictures were taken until I left school and got a job.

Captured on camera in Aberystwyth is one of Tunnel Cement's large fleet of AEC Mammoth Major eight-wheelers. This example, KXY 233, dates from 1949 and is in the early light grey livery with green signwriting.

Another petrol tanker, this time a BMC 701 dating from 1956, in the bright yellow National Benzole livery. The picture was taken in Swansea in June 1957.

This 1949 AEC Monarch, KJJ 118, is in the well-known green and red livery of Shell-Mex, and was photographed in the station car park at Aberystwyth about September 1955.

There was another problem that arose in my particular case - I was brought up in rural Wales where there were few lorries. You'd be lucky to see more than two or three in a day. Ironically I was born but a stone's throw from Spring Place, Kentish Town, London, where General Roadways and later British Road Services were based.

The Luftwaffe was denied the opportunity of getting me as I was whisked away, at the tender age of six months, to the safety of Cardiganshire, where my father had relatives.

Despite the scarcity of lorries and funds, I actually succeeded in getting a few interesting pictures, mainly when visiting towns like Aberystwyth or Swansea. I also begged rides on lorries belonging to J D James, the local haulage contractor, to far off places like Liverpool and Manchester.

Sadly, these were usually on occasions when there wasn't a camera available. Even when I did take a camera I usually messed up the pictures! I just wish I had those times over again.

There was one other obstacle to taking lorry pictures - as soon as drivers saw a camera they thought you were up to no good. I was warned off so many times that I became very wary of taking shots if the driver could see me. I even ended up taking pictures from the three-quarter rear

Parked for the night at Cardiff in the late Fifties, this impressive Scammell Rigid Eight belonged to Johnson and Phillips, the cable makers. The 1953-registered vehicle has Scammell's four-spring rear bogie as opposed to the usual rubber suspension. The livery was dark blue with white lettering.

One of the many contractors engaged on the construction of the first southern section of the M1 motorway in 1958 was Stuart Macey, of High Wycombe. The lorries were worked hard transporting thousands of tons of spoil from one section to another as numerous cuttings and embankments were built to eliminate steep gradients. The nicely proportioned light grey AEC Mammoth Major Mk III tipper (SPP 67) with red mudguards, seen in Park Street, Luton, had evidently lost its offside headlamp lens.

Also photographed during the same visit to Swansea was this superb AEC Mammoth Major Mk III in the famous Silver Roadways livery. Silver Roadways was a subsidiary of Tate and Lyle. The vehicle is fleet number 38 but the registration number is unclear. It appears to be NLV 89 but is a little too blurred to decipher. Anyone with Silver Roadways fleet details who can confirm 38's registration number, please write in and let us know!

view so I couldn't be spotted. Of course such pictures are useless. Now I wish I had had the courage to shoot from the front and be damned.

It was many years before I met anyone else who took lorry photos. I had almost got to wondering if I was some sort of weirdo. However, I carried on and by the time I left Wales to seek my fortune in Luton in 1957 I had a modest photo collection on which to build.

Luton in the 1950s was a busy industrial town dominated by the giant Vauxhall Motors factory where I began work as an apprentice. Funds were still a big problem - my weekly wage of £3 10s hardly covered my digs, so lorry photography was well outside my budget. Once again, I had to content myself with sketching my favourite

wagons and noting the registration numbers, fleet numbers and liveries.

There was certainly no shortage of wagons - hundreds of tons of steel, sheet and coils, came into the factory every day, carried by just about every wellknown haulier from South Wales and the surrounding counties. The likes of the Steel Company of Wales, Richard Thomas and Baldwins, Isaac Caswell, Blue Line, George Read, BRS, Edwards of Lydbrook, Hills of Dinas Powys, and a host of others were to be seen daily.

Then there were others from North Wales and the North West, such as Sealand District Transport, the transport arm of John Summers. Lorries came from all over - Yorkshire, Scotland, the Midlands, you name it!

After a year or so, I borrowed the scruffy folding Kodak camera off my father (who was still living in Wales) and made a more concerted effort to get some pictures. Financial restraints and fear of getting into trouble with drivers limited what I could take, but I did manage to get a few nice shots on occasions.

In total I only took about 200 lorry photos between 1955 and 1960 and a good proportion of those were of poor quality or from silly angles. Still, we've all got to start somewhere!

So it went, until I was lucky enough to meet a gentleman by the name of Arthur Ingram in 1962. I was amazed to discover that I wasn't the only 'truck nut' on the planet. By that time I had bought a second hand camera of my own. This was a Norca

Photographed at Esso's depot in Lampeter station yard in May 1957 is this 1955 Bedford SLC petrol tanker. It was powered by Bedford's 300 cu in petrol engine.

One of the less common types of rigid eight-wheeler was the Guy Invincible Mk 1, using an AEC Mk III chassis with a Gardner engine and David Brown gearbox. It featured a Willenhall steel cab originally designed for ERF but also used by BMC and Dennis. This fine example dating from 1956 is in the dark green livery of Pilkington's Glass and was photographed in Dunstable in 1958.

Another firm to put a fleet of tippers on M1 construction work was Roger Constant of Stourport-on-Severn. This 1957 Leyland Octopus 24.O/5 was one of five seemingly bought with the M1 work in mind. All were finished in a dark green livery with cream writing. TAB 180 is seen at Kidney Wood, Luton, in May 1958.

Contractors descended on Luton from all over the country during the building of the M1. Many leading London-based firms were there, such as Richard Biffa, WW Drinkwater, GJ Palmer and, as seen here, Willment of Waterloo. This barren scene is the M1 at Kidney Wood in the early stages of construction. The Leyland Comet ECOS2.2R is fully laden with chalk to be tipped at another section of the route requiring infill.

6x6cm which wasn't all that brilliant. I began saving for something a bit better and eventually bought one of the newly-introduced Canon Dial half-frames which took 72 pictures on a standard 36 exposure roll.

In itself it was the ideal camera for a furtive lorry photographer such as me. It had a one-handed operation thanks to a pistol grip handle and operated a bit like a cine camera. However there was one big drawback that soon led to me trading it in for a normal 35mm.

The problem was that none of the usual developing and printing services could print half-frame negatives. They were all geared to full-frame 35mm. I kept getting prints with soft detail as if they were out of focus. I thought it might be my negatives that were at fault but they were, in fact, perfectly sharp. After only half a dozen rolls or so I traded the Canon Dial in for a Zeiss Werra 1C 35mm.

What a brilliant camera that was. Although it only cost me £14, it had a Carl Zeiss lens of excellent quality. However it had no rangefinder or light meter but I developed a fairly good sense of judgment and managed to get some very good results. I used to judge the distance (say 30ft) and look at the sky and figure out 125th at f 5.6, or what have you, and

Parked in Kimpton Road at the Vauxhall works in March 1959 are two AEC Mammoth Major Mk IIIs belonging to W and J Chatwin, Smethwick, on contract to Birmid Industries. They are XHA 987 and UHA 783, dating from 1955 and 1954 respectively. Birmid was Vauxhall's main supplier of cylinder block castings.

Below: Although I have no record of the actual date, I believe this shot at Hanger Lane on the North Circular Road was taken about 1957. The main intention was to capture the BOC Sentinel disappearing off to the right of the picture, but another lorry got in the way! Anyway, it shows Bedford O and D types plus an old Morris-Commercial so it wasn't entirely wasted.

9

shoot. Of course I sometimes got it wrong but in the main I was getting good, sharp, well-exposed pictures for the first time in my life.

The Werra 1C was of East German origin and had a few quirky features. For example, you wound the film on by turning a ring around the lens and the film went in the opposite way round to most cameras. As a result, the sequence of negatives ran from right to left. A cone-shaped lens cover doubled as a lens hood - you unscrewed it, reversed it and screwed it back on.

The Werra fitted neatly into my coat pocket, which was very handy when sneaking past security men. I was so pleased with my Werra 1C that I later bought another one so that I could take shots in colour and black and white. I wore out the first one - all the figures were worn off the focusing ring and the film advance mechanism had more play in it than the England cricket team.

Bolstered by the knowledge that there were other 'truck nuts' out there, I began to step up my photography like there was no tomorrow. I also spent my holidays visiting haulage yards and busy industrial towns where I knew I could get good lorry pictures.

I have now been taking photographs of lorries for 50 years and I have recently delved into my early negatives from 1955 to 1959, some which are reproduced here.

Technically, they might not be the best but they were taken on relatively crude cameras by a (then) relatively crude photographer. In one or two instances they may well have appeared in other publications, but most have not previously been published.

In part two I will cover the next five years of my experiences in lorry photography and I hope readers will enjoy a few nostalgic memories from the early Sixties.

The A361 at Bloxham in 1958 is the setting for this rather distant shot of an Atkinson S1586 tipper at work with a Barber Greene. The lorry is in the two-tone green livery of the Mountsorrel Granite Group, of Leicester, but the registration number is unclear.

The flame orange eight-wheelers of the Marston Valley Brick Company were a familiar sight in Luton during the late Fifties. This is a 1955 Foden FG6/15, OBM 536, fleet number 97. Marston Valley was absorbed into the London Brick Company in 1971 and any remaining MVBC lorries were re-liveried in LBC colours.

Below: This shot taken in London Road, the main A6 route south from Luton, shows two fully-laden eight-wheelers of Slough based Contract Transport and Supplies. They are loaded with bricks, probably ex-Stewartby. Note the generous amounts of straw, suggesting that the AEC in the foreground is carrying facing bricks. The AEC is a Mk II, GVF 294, dating from 1947, while the second vehicle is a 1951 Foden FG6/15, OKX 929, fleet number 3. CT and S's livery was mid-green cab and body with red wings and chassis.

11

CONFESSIONS OF A TRUCK PHOTOGRAPHER
PART 2

Peter Davies continues his major series on his 50 years of lorry photography. In 1962 Peter discovered he wasn't the only truck nut in the entire universe when he met a kindred spirit - renowned lorry photographer Arthur Ingram.

Above: A 1949 Albion FT3 of Road Services (Caledonian) trundles along Chaloner Street, part of Liverpool's long dock road, on a wet day in September 1964. The railway lines are those of the Mersey Docks and Harbour Board railway, which was still using steam locos.

Meeting my good friend Arthur Ingram in 1962 gave me new confidence. His interest in photographing lorries was as great as mine. Knowing that I wasn't the only truck nut spurred me on to get a better camera and to step up my photography. I got to know Arthur when I was working for Bedford Trucks. A colleague had got hold of a copy of the HCVC magazine, which Arthur was editing, and suggested I got in touch with him. We're still friends today!

The lorries that were about in the Sixties were much the same as those I had admired during the previous decade.

Having grown up with AEC Mk IIIs and Foden FGs, I still wasn't conscious of the impending demise of such machines. They'd always been there and seemed like a permanent part of the transport scene. New lorries that were appearing such as the AEC Mk V and ERF LV were still very traditional in style and every bit as worthy of a picture as their earlier counterparts.

However, British haulage was about to undergo its biggest ever shake-up during the 1960s. From 1964, new weights and dimensions took effect and it soon dawned on me that the good old British eight-leggers that had dominated the scene in the Fifties were disappearing. It became an urgent matter to record all those post-war veterans that were still grafting away during the Sixties.

Everywhere I went I took my trusty

This S20-cabbed Foden eight-wheel tipper of Wm Cooper, Liverpool, was just a year old when photographed near Runcorn, Cheshire, in September 1964.

An early colour shot of one of Express Dairies' large fleet of AEC Mammoth Major milk tankers taken at South Ruislip LDOY in 1960. The vehicle dates from 1950.

Imagine anyone riding like this nowadays - they'd soon be run in by the law! One of a number of ageing Vulcan tippers operated by Newline Motors, Leicester, until the mid-60s.

Zeiss Werra 1C 35mm camera and made it my mission to take every working classic that I came across. I was, of course, particularly anxious to capture the remaining examples from well-known fleets such as Suttons, Holt Lane, Smith of Maddiston and, of course, BRS.

How I wish I'd been born just a few years earlier! By the time I could afford my own camera so many of the real classics like the BRS Maudslay eight-wheelers were already being scrapped. And BRS vehicles were being given new style fleet numbers from the end of 1963 following changes in the organisation. Anyhow, every era has its place in transport history so whenever you start it is worth recording things as they are. Arthur, being 10 years my senior, enjoyed several years recording

Europe in the 1960s was a different world. Antwerp was a good place to see gems like this impressive bonneted Henschel artic - as long as you didn't get arrested in the process!

the scene in North London in the heyday of BRS - lucky fellow!

Truck photography can be quite a challenge in that trucks are on the move all the time. Sometimes you can be lucky enough to find them back at base but often they are hundreds of miles away. The best way of getting good lorry pictures is to hang around industrial areas or main roads and take pot luck.

That's what I decided to do during the Sixties and, for that matter, still do whenever the opportunity arises. My favourite places used to include parts of London, Liverpool and the North West, the Forth-Clyde area and South Wales.

Liverpool in the Sixties was a wonderland of classic haulage wagons - this general view of Regent Road captures the atmosphere well. Long queues of lorries waiting to unload, parked on the old granite setts - to my mind there was nowhere quite like it.

Another view of the Liverpool dock area in 1964. Taken outside Park Lane goods yard, this shot includes an ex-BRS Mk III in Coward Bros livery and one of Edward Derbyshire's superb Leyland Octopus flats loaded with drums from Monsanto.

Doubtless there were other regions, such as Bristol, Hull and the North East, that were equally good, but Liverpool in particular had a certain lure - the seven miles of docks from Crosby in the north to Garston in the south used to be teeming with lorries of all shapes and sizes.

I got in there when there were still lots of real wagons about - wagons you only see in preservation nowadays. In the Sixties they were still hard at work and the scene had not changed very much since the early post-war years.

But suspicion aroused by a bod with a camera was even more of a problem then. How do you explain to an angry driver or an over-zealous Jobsworth security guard that you're just a lorry enthusiast and pose no threat? They automatically think that you're snooping around and intent on causing trouble. Oddly enough, I've never been troubled by the police. They seem to accept that you're not breaking any laws so have no reason to interfere.

But I will never forget an incident involving the Belgian police in 1965. Arthur and I decided we'd venture over the water to see the transport scene in Belgium, Holland and Germany. After all, back then it was a different world, a world of Krupps, Bussings and Henschels. We went on the Transport Ferry Service from

Reminiscent of the 1930s is this classic Scammell Artic 8 seen on London's North Circular Road.

A Mason's of Rotherham Leyland artic grinds slowly up Archway Hill in north London in 1966 as it sets out on its journey back to Yorkshire.

Oh no - caught in the act! A stern-looking approaching security guard has spotted me taking this shot of a 1954 ERF six-wheeler, and I'm about to be given the third degree.

Tilbury to Antwerp, taking my VW van. We were feeling very pleased with ourselves, having taken hundreds of pictures during our week-long expedition.

On the last day, just a few hours before we were due to board the ferry, we were busily taking pictures in the town when the air was filled with sirens and flashing blue lights. Without any explanation we were arrested by armed police and driven off to the nick. There we had our passports and all our possessions impounded and were questioned separately through an interpreter.

It was quite a stressful experience to say the least and the recent case of the plane-spotters in Greece was a vivid reminder. It appears that we had been identified by the staff of a local bank as a pair of bank robbers who were casing the joint. No joke this - they were deadly serious. Interpol were alerted and while we were being held in custody the British police visited our homes in England to investigate. Having proved our innocence and explained our hobby we were eventually released.

It wasn't until we got back home that we found out we were in all the national dailies! My only regret was that we missed a lot of good motors while we were being held in custody.

This Blue Circle Foden FG four-wheel bulk tanker, seen at the company's Houghton Regis, Beds, works in 1965, features the unusual style Redhill cab.

Syd Harrison of Sheffield is still famous for its fantastic fleet of Scammells. They were regular sights at Vauxhall Motors, where they delivered crankshaft forgings for Ambrose Shardlow. This shot dates from November 1964.

Waiting to unload at the Co-op Dairy in Manor Road, Luton, in 1964 is a 1948 AEC Monarch milk tanker.

A Liverpool-based Albion HD57 flat from the Guinness fleet parked along the dock road in 1964.

CONFESSIONS
OF A TRUCK
PHOTOGRAPHER
PART 3

Confessions moves into colour for this third instalment of Peter Davies's reminiscences of 50 years of truck photography!

As the Sixties unfolded my photographic efforts gained momentum and everywhere I went, my trusty Zeiss Werra 1C went with me. Black and white photography was still accepted as the norm while colour was regarded as an exciting new medium to be reserved for special occasions.

Special occasions to many people are holidays and weddings, but to me they were visits to haulage yards and industrial towns.

I had tried colour photography some years earlier using my 6x6cm camera but the results were disappointing for a number of reasons. I soon realised that you had to be much more precise with the exposure settings, especially for colour transparencies. There was little latitude; if you got it wrong your slides could be pale and milky or as dark as night.

Another difficulty in those days was that colour film was much slower - less sensitive to light - than black and white, so it meant shooting at slower shutter speeds and wider apertures (larger lens openings). The practical effect of this was to increase the risk of fuzzier pictures, because of camera shake and subject movement, and the smaller range of sharp focus from the wide aperture.

In 45 years amateur photography has come a long way. Nowadays it's possible to shoot on fine grain high speed colour film in cameras which set the exposure accurately and focus automatically.

Of course, if you have really moved into the 21st Century you use a digital camera. There's a lot to be said for the new technology but I'm so geared to the old system that I still use conventional film.

Anyway, back to the Sixties, the colour

Pickfords Tank Haulage Atkinson artic with 150 Gardner photographed at the Border Café near Wrexham in 1964.

AE Morris of Handsworth, Birmingham, was absorbed into Smith of Maddiston in 1961 when the Falkirk firm was expanding rapidly. This S20 eight-wheel flat, seen near the Jungle Café, is in the cream, maroon and red Smith livery. The nearside front tyre had seen better days! Perhaps that's the new one on top of the load

This is one to fox most people. No, it's not a Scammell. Nor is it a modified Foden DG. It is actually one of a small number of home-made ballast tractors built by Union Cartage for local dock work and is seen crossing Tower Bridge in 1964.

Ex-BRS AEC Mammoth Major Mk III was part of the Browns of Beverley fleet and is seen here unloading at Vauxhall Motors in February 1966. Browns delivered shock absorbers for Armstrong Patents

results, not surprisingly, were somewhat unpredictable. Ektachrome E3 film was quite expensive but I was able to get it at a good discount. Colour processing was more expensive than black and white but the attraction of seeing my favourite wagons in glorious Technicolor led me to switch to colour about 1965 when there were still many of the old traditional liveries still about.

I'm so glad I did, I was able to record many of my favourite liveries, such as Suttons, Holt Lane, Smith of Maddiston and Henry Long. Just as precious were the leading own-account fleets such as Cement Marketing Co, Ranks Flour, Tate and Lyle and so on.

Truck photography is not without its ups and downs and for every triumph there's a disaster. I've had quite a few of the latter. Once my camera fell off the passenger seat of my van when I pulled up a bit sharply and unbeknown to me the impact dislodged the prism in the viewfinder.

Several rolls later I discovered that all my pictures were half missing. I had been carefully framing the lorries as usual but

Greenwoods of St Ives, Hunts, ran a fine fleet of AECs in brown with black wings and red wheels. WEW 208 was hastily captured on camera in 1964 on Tower Bridge just as a Vauxhall PA Cresta tried to get in the way

If I was asked to nominate my favourite shot of all time, this blockbuster from Henry Long is a real contender. Fifties trailer outfits don't come much better than this.

James and Alexander Smith, better known as Smith of Maddiston, had one of Scotland's finest liveries which survived the United takeover in 1966 but did not appeal to a South African manager who was drafted in during the late Seventies. He changed it, introducing more cream and a restyled logo which was singularly uninspiring. I'm glad I got this Mk V on record while the "proper" livery was still in use.

Impressive or what? A 32-ton drawbar outfit of Sammy Williams, fully laden with steel, crawls up the hill past Hayward Tyler on the approach to Vauxhall Motors in 1964.

Riley's had one of the first Guy Invincible Mk 2s, 5764 WE, seen here parked in Bridge Street lorry park, Luton, near the town centre. This shot actually dates from 1959.

Riley's of Birley Vale, Sheffield, were a regular sight in Luton where they had a depot. The maroon fleet included gems like this Bonallack ECOS2.1R Comet dropside.

they all came out with either the cabs or the back ends chopped off. I lost at least a couple of hundred shots, including some cracking eight-leggers.

During that period I had paid visits to Liverpool and Manchester and spent time on the A1 as well as on the motorway services.

I visited so many haulage yards in the Sixties and by and large people were very helpful. Only on a few occasions was I met with refusal. One particularly disappointing refusal was at a yard which ran some impressive tackle including eight-wheelers and trailers and some twin-steer tractors which were cut down eight-wheelers. However, I later discovered that they had been in trouble with the Traffic Commissioners.

I would often telephone firms or write to them asking if I could take pictures. I wrote to one firm that used to operate some beautifully liveried Fodens, Joseph Roscoe, of Westhoughton, Bolton. The answer was "Yes", so I paid them a visit. They were still running a lovely old DG6/15 flat which, luckily, was at the depot.

The boss had even got one of his workshop staff to go round it with a paintbrush and the paint on the mudguards was still wet. It made it look a bit artificial but I hadn't the heart to tell him!

Late evening on Barnet Hill in fading light. You had to have a steady hand to capture the night trunkers heading out of London. Here's one of Sutton's classic eight-wheel Atkis, sheeted and roped to perfection.

Marvellous old FG6/15 of Marley Tiles photographed near Hexham, Northumberland, at the end of the Sixties decade, when such machines were already beginning to be phased out.

I won't apologise for taking so many AECs and Fodens - they were regarded as some of the best British lorries of the Sixties when I shot this lovely old Mk V flat at Smiles' yard in Bleucher, Newcastle-on-Tyne.

One of the last firms to operate Sentinel DVs was W L Duffield, of Saxlingham Thorpe, Norfolk. JOA 391 was photographed at their mill in July 1966.

Superb old Fletcher Miller Mk III tanker on 900x24s parked in Kimpton Road, Luton, in September 1966. OLG 501 was new to the Hyde, Cheshire, oil distributor in 1951.

Undoubtedly one of the best liveried and best turned out own-account fleets was that of Tate and Lyle. These stocky, well-proportioned bulk granulated sugar tankers were among my favourite wagons. This is a blower discharge version captured on camera in Queen's Drive, Liverpool, in 1967.

Click, and another famous livery goes on record. This is one of Spillers' distinctive Albion HD57s parked at the Millennium Mill, Silvertown, London. Like a fool I didn't photograph the Kew Dodge!

Mr Roscoe got one of his workshop staff to paint the wheels and mudguards of this magnificent old DG eight-wheeler when I turned up to take its picture in December 1966. The paint was still wet!

CONFESSIONS OF A TRUCK PHOTOGRAPHER

PART 4

Peter Davies continues the story of his 50 years of lorry photography by remembering his job with Bedford's publicity department.

Vehicles that are now regarded as sought-after classics were still plentiful in the 'seventies. A good example is this Guy Big J8 tipper seen at Brent Cross in September 1970. D J Light was based at Bath.

Drivers in the 'seventies were a pretty hardy lot. This brave soul had lost his windscreen but was evidently unperturbed and carried on regardless. The 1968 Big J8 loaded with coal was snapped at Brent Cross in 1970.

To someone who was brought up in rural Wales, Luton was a hive of industry. With industry goes transport, so there was no shortage of lorries to keep an enthusiast happy. Working at a truck manufacturer was the icing on the cake. My job was in the publicity department which was allied to the sales department.

To produce sales brochures and advertising, one needs pictures so I made it known from an early stage that I could contribute my talents in this area. While the actual photography was usually carried out by professionals with expensive cameras, someone was needed to liaise with dealers and transport firms to fix up the jobs. It's a responsibility that suited me nicely.

Dealers used to tip me off when an interesting new Bedford was being delivered and I would fix up the photography and act as creative director. It meant travelling to many of the industrial areas that I used to frequent on my personal lorry expeditions.

Inevitably one saw other interesting motors on such travels and consequently I got some good shots of the competition as well as Bedfords.

I also used to fix up all the photography on new models as they came out. I was thus privileged to drive all the new prototypes such as the KMs and TMs, often borrowing trailers from the likes of York at Northallerton and Crane Fruehauf at Dereham. I thoroughly enjoyed such exercises as I could get out on the road.

To get good truck shots, it pays to be interested in trucks as you can then get the best out of the subject. Finding a suitable

Not only have Seddons disappeared from the scene since this shot was taken in September 1970 but once famous fleets like that of bulk liquid specialists Bulwark Transport have gone too.

What was ultra modern back in the 'seventies has now become historic. This fully freighted AEC 'Ergo' eight-wheeler is a superb specimen of a type now only seen at rallies. This Redland example was brand new when photographed at the Target roundabout on the A40 in 1970.

location and choosing the right viewpoint come with experience. It is also important to ensure that details on the vehicle are right, such as correctly adjusted mirrors.

I set high standards in Bedford photography, something that was appreciated by the company, and I was even asked to write a detailed guide to truck photography for use by international GM dealers and advertising agencies.

The world of photography and advertising is commonly thought of as glamorous but often it is anything but. One typical shoot I recall, in January 1968, was fraught with problems from beginning to end, some of which I must admit were of my own making.

Our advertising agency was briefed to produce an ad to promote the Bedford KM tipper as a rugged machine for site work.

Finding a location was left to the agency

The likes of Ford D Series and Bedford TKs were regarded as 'run of the mill' machines but sometimes appeared with axle conversions which changed them into sought-after gems like this impressive 'Chinese Six' of Ivy House Products from Audlem in Cheshire.

Some celebrated liveries were still to be seen in the early 'seventies including that of A M Walker of Leicester. The traditional green and red on this 1966 Atkinson Silver Knight was soon to be replaced by a plain orange treatment.

and my job was to turn up at the appointed time with a fully-laden KM tipper. Our demonstration fleet included a D-reg KMR but, at that point, it was out on loan to a dealer in Cumbria.

The agency found a suitable location on the Kingston By-pass in Surrey, where a new flyover was being built, and they decided that it would be quite dramatic to do a night shot.

Could this be a preserved ERF parked up on grass at a rally? No! – this fine 6.8GX from Bardon Hill Quarries was waiting to tip tarmac at road works near Stafford in July 1971.

Sometimes what promises to be a superb shot of a classic can be marred by poor quality film. The colours and general quality in this shot of Robson's 'Border Volunteer', an S39 Foden artic, were disappointing. However the 1970 lorry is a real gem and a poor shot is better than no shot at all.

Brand new and looking pristine is this 32-ton Scammell Trunker of coal haulier Garratt & Hemphrey of Nottingham. At the time it was seen as a real leviathan of the roads. By today's standards, of course, it is quite modest with a payload of around 18-19 tons.

Many enthusiasts will have seen 604GXV at rallies since it was saved for preservation by Charles Roads. This shot shows the 1963 Foden S20 sugar tanker in its working days, caught on camera at Watford Gap Services in July 1971.

The tipper was due back that afternoon, giving me just enough time to get it loaded with seven yards of hogging and to meet the agency people in Richmond by 7.15pm.

On the appointed afternoon it was pouring with rain and it was already beginning to get dark when the demonstrator finally arrived back at 3.45pm. It was filthy and had one rear light out, which I had to fix. The pit was 10 miles away along country lanes and the digger driver went home at 5 o'clock. It didn't stop raining and Three Hills Pit at Codicote was like a severe cross-country course, much

of it under several inches of muddy water.

Where I loaded must have been a mile from the entrance and just navigating my way back to the main road was quite a challenge in the dark. Anyway I got to the rendezvous point at Richmond bang on time. There I was met by an anxious agency rep, who announced that the photographer had been rushed to hospital with appendicitis and they were frantically trying to find a stand-in. Meanwhile I was parked for an hour on a steep hill in a narrow road in the town.

In due course we made our way to the construction site. Thankfully the rain eased off long enough for the photographer to do his stuff. The session dragged on until one o'clock in the morning, by which time I just wanted to get home and get to bed. What

was to be done with the load of wet hogging? The agency had paid for it but weren't too bothered what became of it once the photo session was over.

By coincidence, I was in the process of laying a hard standing on which to park my old Maudslay and had already gathered about 20 tons of hardcore which needed blinding off with the very stuff I had now inherited.

By 2.30am I was back home in Luton and the rain had come on again. I decided I would tip the hogging there and then and backed off the main road into the end of my garden. Unfortunately, in the dark, I got stuck in the soft ground and ended up having to call out the recovery boys. Needless to say they weren't too pleased at that unearthly hour! What was supposed to be a freebie worked out rather expensive at the end of the day.

The epilogue to this saga was itself quite amusing. One of the shots appeared in a press advertisement in the News of the World

Volvo F86s were growing in numbers in the 'seventies after British operators had sampled the comfort and ease of driving that made them great favourites. The unassuming Swedish newcomers soon began to outnumber some of their British contemporaries. This Manchester registered Co-op flour tanker dates from 1970 and was photographed near Tower Bridge in August of that year.

Scania paralleled Volvo with its forward-control tractors aimed at the UK market in the 'seventies. Once they got a foothold with impressive machines like this '111' of P & O Roadways they never looked back. Drivers loved them and basked in the glamour they brought to the job.

One can sometimes get an excellent vehicle-to-vehicle 'tracking' shot but it pays to be discreet about it! This nice ERF 6.8GXB flat of F R Somerset was snapped as it pounded up the M1 in Nottinghamshire in 1980.

Another 'foreign' make to enter the UK scene in the 'seventies was DAF. Like other European trucks they were first seen as curiosities but thirty years on they have ousted all the Brits. T Brady & Son of Barrow-in-Furness operated this nicely liveried 1974 2600 photographed at Toddington Services in 1980.

Bedford fought bravely for a share of the max-cap market with their Detroit Diesel-powered TM. This sleeper-cabbed TM 3800 had the 8V-71 two-stroke diesel and sounded really great. However poor fuel consumption was a drawback.

ERF fought back against the European manufacturers with its B-series launched in 1974. They could give any foreign competition a run for their money and it is sad that ERF has now all but vanished.

and the agency received an inquiry from a lady reader who wanted to contact the handsome driver of the truck! Perhaps what she really needed was a new pair of glasses.

The Seventies was an interesting era for me - the launch of the TM was particularly exciting. Most of the traditional truck manufacturers were still in existence. Sadly the rot was beginning to set in as many makes were killed off within British Leyland and the European imports were growing in numbers.

I made sure I photographed as many of the Seventies classics as I could, including ERF A and B series, AEC Ergos, Marathons, Foden S80s, Atki Borderers and Seddon 400s while they were still plentiful.

Of course I made sure I shot plenty of Volvos and Scanias too - they were all part of the British scene in the Seventies. It's a sobering thought that all those motors have vanished, save for a few seen on the rally fields.

Leyland's answer to the European competition was the Marathon launched in August 1973. This one of F Horne & Sons from Bishop Auckland was one of the first that I photographed and was brand new when this shot was taken at Toddington Services in 1974.

While Borderers are among the most popular of preserved trucks their rear-steer counterparts, known as Leaders, were less common. They were only built from 1970-1972. Moreton C Cullimore of Stroud operated this fine example photographed on a sunny day along the Grosvenor Road in London.

This is the advertising shot promoting the KMR as a tough site tipper. It was taken on a wet night at a flyover construction site on the Kingston Bypass. The truck was D registered but the agency retouched the D to an F to bring it up to date as the ad was released in 1968.

CONFESSIONS OF A TRUCK PHOTOGRAPHER PART V

Peter Davies investigates the joy of trucks in Europe as part of this latest instalment recalling his 50 years of lorry photography.

Below: A pair of Tayforth Group Seddon 32:4 artics with consecutive reg nos, RSD208M and RSD207M, parked up at Toddington Services in August 1975. Tayforth was part of the National Freight Corporation along with BRS.

T hroughout my years of photographing trucks there have been the odd occasions when I have thought "that's it, I've taken enough pictures of all my favourite wagons so I'll cut down and be a bit more selective". Of course that doesn't last long – there's always something new that's worth a shot.

Sometimes when looking through my files I see lorries in the background of pictures and think "why the hell didn't I take that?" I realise just how many cracking motors I didn't bother to take. Stuff like Scania LB76s, Atkinson Borderers and Scammell Crusaders. Still, you can't take everything – it would be far too expensive in film alone!

Having had a taste of European trucks in the mid-60s I was eager to get more. Our Product Information Department at Vauxhall Motors had copies of 'Inufa' (the comprehensive all-make buyers guide for European trucks) and, having begged one or two old copies, I became fascinated by some of the eight-leggers which were appearing in Switzerland and Italy. Spain was another country known to have eight-wheelers. Italian and Spanish eight-wheelers, unlike the Brits, were adaptations of Chinese Sixes, having add-on self-steering tag axles. British eight-wheelers were of course normal six-wheelers with a second steer added.

An excellent opportunity came up in 1977 when my boss instructed me to deliver a new TM3800 down to the Barcelona Show. I took plenty of film with me and hoped to get a shot of the odd Pegaso or Barreiros eight-legger. I just hadn't realised how common they were. They easily outnumbered artics and I ended up taking hundreds of shots. Not only were there loads of Spanish-built trucks but there were some fantastic old Brits about too, such as Super Beavers with third axles and bonneted Leyland Comets. Some of those magnificent old Super Beavers carried

Scammell Crusaders were something of a status symbol in their day – real "men's motors". This 1974 example from Hughes Haulage, Llanelli was photographed in their yard in April 1976. Hughes Bros was part of Blue Dart Transport, which was in turn a wholly owned subsidiary of British Vita of Middleton, Manchester.

A visit to Richards & Osborne's Fraddon yard in Cornwall in 1976 yielded this fine example of an ERF 6.8GXB bulk tipper. Pity the 'F' had disappeared from the grille badge!

At the time I regarded this shot as a real scoop – it was my first sighting of a new Sedak 400 in an operator's livery, in this case Bowater Scott. The shot dates from October 1975.

Parcel carriers J Brevitt of Willenhall operated a nicely liveried fleet of TKs on C and D work. The company also ran Fodens on long distance under the 'Hall Transport' name but in the same red and cream colours.

I was pleasantly surprised at the large numbers of eight-leggers to be seen in Spain in the '70s. This superb Pegaso '1066' model seen in Bilbao had a 24-ton payload capacity – equal to the gross weight of some UK eight-wheelers.

Ford's big Transcontinentals were appearing in the mid-70s. This one, in the colours of Henry Telfer Ltd, was an early example caught on camera at Toddington Services in September 1976.

'El Camion Ingles' badges.

A few months later I was given the job of delivering another TM to the Turin Show and managed to get some interesting Italian stuff. That trip wasn't as fruitful though, as it was in October and the weather wasn't very good.

The sameness that has extended across the European Union in recent years had not taken hold back then. There was still a lot of variety to be found in the trucks

When you think you've exhausted all the UK possibilities there's plenty of different trucks to be found abroad. At least there was in the 1970s. A trip to Turin in October 1977 yielded this spectacular Fiat 44-tonne 8-axle drawbar outfit parked on the Italian side of the Mont Blanc Tunnel.

The urge to find new types of eight-wheelers lured me to Switzerland in 1981 where the likes of this Saurer 5DF 8x4 were quite plentiful. They were built to 2.3m (7ft 6in) wide and had exceptionally long rear overhangs. This example appears to be Italian owned.

'El Camion Ingles' - a most impressive Leyland Super Beaver six-wheeler caught on camera near the dock area of Barcelonetta in April 1977.

Underfloor-engined Büssings were always a great favourite of mine as were British Sentinels. When I was fortunate enough to spend some time in Frankfurt in 1979 there were still loads of Büssings to be seen on the autobahns.

of different nations. Germany, which I visited for the 1979 Frankfurt Show, still favoured drawbar outfits. Eight-wheelers were virtually unknown even on construction work. All the same, I was able to get some really good truck pictures while there were still loads of Büssings, Krupps and Hanomag Henschels to be seen along the autobahns.

I still wanted to witness some of those nice Saurer, Berna and FBW eight-wheelers in Switzerland at first hand so in the early '80s I borrowed a motor caravan and took my wife and two daughters on a tour of Switzerland and Italy. I managed to get some excellent shots but my family were far from pleased with me as I got a bit carried away and almost forgot it that it was their holiday too!

These were the first of many sorties to other countries to get interesting truck pictures. Though keen to photograph 'foreigners' I have never neglected British lorries – they are still my number one

Old established wet grains merchant James & Sons, once famous for their unique Ford drawbar outfits, had progressed on to 32-ton artics by 1979 when this Foden S83 outfit was photographed at Toddington Services.

DEMONSTRATION VEHICLE

LEYLAND

CAFFYNS LTD

GNJ 244V

This year the Leyland Roadtrain celebrated its 25th birthday. When this demonstrator outfit was caught on film in March 1980 it was the hottest news on the truck scene.

interest and I like to get new stuff when it first comes out. Stuff, in years gone by, like the new Leyland Roadtrain which first took to the roads in 1980.

Just recently Roadtrain enthusiasts celebrated 25 years of the marque. It started me off looking through my Leyland pictures and I found some good shots of T45s taken during the '80s and '90s. It's strange to think that such vehicles are now virtually extinct and I'm so glad that I photographed plenty of

them when they were at work. In the '70s we said goodbye to several major British marques including Guy, Albion and AEC. In the '80s Britain's transport

scene was to undergo even more drastic change with the disappearance of more famous makes including Scammell and Bedford.

Nowadays Dennis only build specialist vehicles such as refuse trucks and airport trucks but one could still see Dennis lorries around in the early '80s even though they were quite rare compared with other makes. This smart curtainsider was operated by the Yorkshire Bottle Co of Bawtry and dates from 1977.

I came to realise that you could never really run out of subjects in the UK. Gems like this ERF B-series curtainsider were always worth a shot. This beauty was part of the Whitworths Foods fleet based at Wellingborough.

CONFESSIONS OF A TRUCK PHOTOGRAPHER
PART 6

The law, as dictated by one Mr Murphy, has many times cast its murky shadow of unpredictability over Peter Davies' truck photography!

Below: Curses! It's that phantom pedestrian of old London Town! What promised to be a nice shot of a BRS Bristol HA6L artic was marred by the sudden appearance of this casual passer-by. A classic example of Murphy's Law.

Taking pictures of lorries is a doddle or so you might think. There are thousands of motors out there just waiting to be captured on camera. But is it really as easy as that? Not if you are only after certain types in certain operators' liveries. There's a completely unpredictable phenomenon known as 'Murphy's Law'.

It works like this – you wait at the roadside for hours hoping to spot the specific vehicle you want and, however hard you try, it eludes you. When you pack it in and drive off empty-handed the very vehicle you've been waiting for suddenly appears, usually on the opposite carriageway!

Alternatively you can be driving along and you see one superb truck after another going by. You find a convenient stopping place and wait there in eager anticipation. You wait and wait only to find that all the good lorries have mysteriously vanished. It's a bit like trying to win the lottery – the odds are very much against you doing so.

On many occasions I have resorted to chasing a lorry for miles in order to get a picture. Having spotted something good heading the opposite way I have done a 'U-ey' and gone like a bat out of hell to catch and overtake it so that I can park further down the road and grab a shot as it goes by. If it's really good I have leapfrogged it several times to get a series of shots. Sometimes I was lucky but on other occasions I pursued lorries in vain, losing the trail at a junction or roundabout.

To get the perfect shot a whole number of different factors have to come together – location, light, a fully functioning camera, film and of course the lorry itself. Often one or more of these factors is lacking. There are occasions when you're in the perfect location with excellent light with a perfectly adjusted camera loaded with the right sort of film but no decent lorries appear. At other times you can find a superb lorry in a lousy location with a lamppost in the way or with a car partially

28

One way to get good pictures is to wait at the roadside and hope some decent lorries come along. It's a bit of a lottery but sometimes you strike lucky with gems like this Seddon 32:4 of Walls Ice Cream seen on the old A5 in June 1969.

For real atmosphere you can't beat the old dock areas like Liverpool. This Stanley's of Oldham Seddon six-wheeler was photographed within North Gladstone Branch Dock when plod wasn't looking. The picture dates from April 1972.

My all time favourite haulage livery is that of Sam Anderson of Newhouse. I was gutted when Murphy's Law reared its ugly head just as I was about to shoot this tasty Mk.V. A grotty Thames Trader tipper and an A-series Bedford got in the way.

I particularly like shooting trucks in urban settings but fewer and fewer opportunities exist today as most towns are by-passed. This Atkinson Silver Knight Mk.II of Spiers & Hartwell was captured on camera as it rounded a tight corner in Evesham in April 1975.

obscuring it.

Alternatively everything might be perfect except for the light – for instance bright sunlight might be shining straight into the lens. Equally frustrating are the occasions when you spot a superb lorry heading your way and you think nothing can go wrong. Everything is right including the location and the light and, horror of horrors, you've just come to the end of the film and you don't have time to reload.

Then of course there are cyclists and pedestrians who suddenly get in the way

just as you're about to take the shot of a lifetime. Yes, Murphy's Law has a lot to answer for. Even though a picture can be spoiled by poor light, poor location or by a passing car it is worth keeping it if only for future reference. It might be the only shot you ever get of the vehicle in question and a poor shot is better than no

shot at all.

There's another 'wild card' factor which can scupper your chances – the casual, inquisitive or obstructive bystander. A classic instance occurred one evening on Barnet Hill when I'd set out to get a shot of Richardson's (Hull) Transport's AEC Mk.III drawbar outfit. Having waited some time for the lorry to appear I was approached by a bloke who'd broken down in a Heinkel bubble car. Could I give him a push? How embarrassing is that! Of course, while I was dutifully helping him out the very lorry I was

When the bubble car owner robbed me of the Richardson's (Hull) Transport Mk.III (see text), this Mk.V which was following helped make up for the loss. Look at that load – that's what a proper sheeted load looks like!

I broke down on the hard shoulder on the M1 just after overtaking this superb Mammoth Major Mk.V drawbar outfit. Damn me if I didn't break down again about a mile up the road enabling me to get a second shot.

Backlit shots can work out well provided you don't get the sun shining right into the lens. By keeping the camera in the shadow of the building this shot of a Scammell Routeman II in Hull turned out a real winner.

Above: Finding good locations and taking pot luck on a truck coming along is a bit of a gamble. So much the better if you can pre-arrange the whole thing. That's exactly what I did with this British registered Dennison eight-wheeler. The owners, P R Bushell of Halkyn in North Wales, kindly posed the truck in a quarry and even got the loader to perform – such was the importance of getting a good shot of this rare machine.

waiting for drove past and I missed it.

On another occasion I was just lining up to get a nice shot of an ERF eight-wheel bulk powder tanker just inside the dock gates in Liverpool when the police on the gate spotted me. "Have you got a photography permit", asked the cop. "No", I replied with all honesty. I was told "Put your camera away". As he turned away I grabbed a quick shot but his mate spotted me. "Do that again", he says, "and the next photo will be of you – down at the nick". At this point I beat a hasty retreat.

I suppose it must be difficult for the average person to understand lorry enthusiasts. You're immediately suspected of having a sinister motive even though your intentions are perfectly innocent. Despite the existence of enthusiasts' clubs and magazines, Joe Public is unaware that our hobby even exists.

I raced down a mountain pass with hairpin bends to overtake this rare Swiss registered OM eight-wheeler back in August 1982. It was a nail-biting experience. Having screeched to a halt I leapt out just in time to catch it as it went by. Phew!

Left: If you like big trucks, Sweden is worth a visit. Drawbar rigs like this Volvo F12 Globetrotter measure up to 24m in length and weigh around 52tonnes gross. This shot was taken near Karlstad in May 1981.

Location can make or break a picture. With a backdrop as nice as this you can't fail. Everything fits together perfectly in this shot of a CMC Scammell Routeman III taken at Houghton Regis Cement Works in June 1974.

Congested town centres can provide an interesting setting. Ampthill is a small Georgian market town with narrow streets. This shot of a Tunnel Cement AEC artic was taken in 1978, just before the new by-pass opened. An elderly lady beamed approval when she saw me taking pictures and said, "It's time someone did something about these awful lorries."

One can't always find a scenic background but it does help. In this case a Russian built MAZ 504A articulated bulk cement tanker was photographed along the picturesque bank of the Danube in Budapest.

Right: A warm sunny day might be ideal for taking truck photos but, sometimes, adverse weather can be turned to good effect. I was very pleased with this shot of a C Herring B-series artic taken during a heavy snowstorm in Liverpool in 1982.

A nice winding road with a scenic background – just the sort of place to get a good shot. I set up here on the A74 in October 1991 and was pleased to get this shot of two Eddie Stobart Stratos.

CONFESSIONS OF A TRUCK PHOTOGRAPHER PART 7

Peter Davies brings the story of his 50 years of lorry photography up to date, emphasises the need for a proper filing system and even flirts with digital!

Automotive Products of Leamington Spa used to deliver Lockheed brake components to motor manufacturers with this Dodge 300 series, seen here at Vauxhall Motors in 1965. The lorry is in their old light brown livery which was soon to be replaced by a rather stark black and white scheme.

The Austin FJ had the distinction of being one of the first British trucks to feature a tilt cab as standard. This nicely proportioned dropsider has a third axle conversion and is in the smart blue livery of H Welch of West Bromwich.

It's all very well taking loads of lorry pictures but as your collection builds up you need a way of storing them. You get past the stage where an old shoe box will do to store all those little yellow Kodak wallets. Admittedly up to a certain point you don't really need a sophisticated storage and retrieval system because you can remember exactly what you've got. In my teens, all I needed was one of those family photo albums with a mock crocodile skin cover so I could spend hours pasting in all those fuzzy little contact prints, each suitably captioned with the make and type.

At first it didn't seem so important to record dates and locations as I knew them all off by heart. It's not until the collection reaches thousands that you realise how important such details are. One good thing about modern digital cameras is that all this vital information is recorded automatically.

At the end of the day there's no substitute for meticulous record keeping. Over the years your memory can let you down. Just this year I was approached by a keen enthusiast at the Trans Pennine Run who queried a caption I had written. "You say that the R Hanson Atkinson eight-wheeler on such and such a page in your book was photographed in Barnsley", he said. "I've studied the photo and it doesn't look like Barnsley". When I checked back he was

A 1969 ERF 6.6GX six-wheeled flat in Hargreaves Transport's colours. It has a Gardner 150 and the 2LV(M) cab and is a true classic of the 'sixties era. Hargreaves was based in Cannock.

Athersmith Bros of Barrow-in-Furness were loyal Seddon customers throughout their history. This 1963 registered six-wheeler was photographed in Hitchin in July 1965. Athersmiths, who did a lot of work for Bowaters Paper, were later absorbed into that other well-known Barrow-in-Furness fleet, T Brady & Sons.

One of Britain's best known tipper fleets was that of Hoveringham Gravels who were noted for their Foden S21 'Mickey Mouse' eight-leggers with Neville U-shaped bodies. KNN616E was captured on camera at Brigg, Lincolnshire in June 1971.

Much was made of the 'angle planned' doors of the Morris 'Threepenny Bit'. Safety was the objective but ironically there was nothing to stop the driver stepping out in front of other traffic! This Lyons Bakery van is pictured in a busy High Street setting – exactly the conditions for which it was designed.

right – the lorry was photographed in Derby! I had recorded the date and location but had been too lazy to check.

It was in the mid-'sixties that I began logging my pictures in greater detail, giving each shot a reference number and listing the date, location, make, type and operator. This system worked well and was adhered to for fifteen years but it was time-consuming so I switched to keeping a summary of the pictures on each roll whilst still allocating numbers to each frame. An efficient filing system is vitally important. Without one it would be virtually impossible to locate a specific shot from tens of thousands on file.

At one time, with the help of a computer buff I knew, I began to enter my pictures on computer but after five thousand or so I decided the idea was too time-consuming. In recent years I have scanned hundreds of my old pictures which are now safely stored on computer and backed up on CDs. Computers have opened up completely new opportunities and I sometimes wonder how I ever managed without one.

Before computers and scanners came within reach of the individual the only way to supply pictures to publishers was to send the original. I have lost at least a dozen or so important originals at publishers and, once lost, they can never be replaced. All that is a thing of the past – now I simply scan a

Right: What began as a laundry business in Salford near Manchester developed into a thriving truck rental operation known as Salford Van Hire which is still going strong. Here one of their 1975 Ford Transcons is seen on a crisp winter's morning heading south on the A74 in Scotland.

In the early 'seventies, following a relaxation of the 'second man' requirement, there was an upsurge in the use of drawbar outfits. Typical is this fine Cummins engined ERF A-series in the smart livery of Knowles of Wimblington.

The Volvo F88 was seen as the ultimate in long distance wagons in the 'seventies. For comfort and power they were hard to beat and drivers loved them. Nelsons of Arnside, one time big users of AECs and Leylands, operated this example seen at Toddington Services in July 1975.

Below: The recent feature on Mammoth Minors in CVC got me looking through my AEC pictures and I turned up this humdinger of a TIR outfit with sleeper cab conversion. TAK121J was photographed at Scratchwood (now Gateway) Services on the M1 in 1974. Pity it was parked so close to the lorry in front as that cast a shadow over the grille. Was it Murphy's Law at work again?

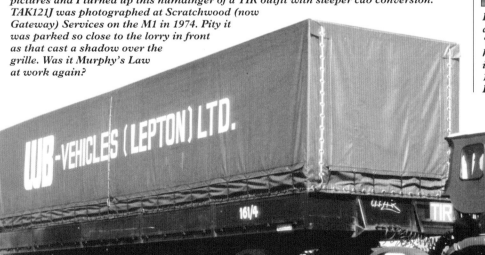

picture and email it or, if there are several, put them on a CD.

Digital photography is undoubtedly the way to go. I recently tried out a digital SLR – a Nikon D70 – and was very impressed, not only with the convenience of having immediate results but with the quality of the images and the fact that hundreds of shots can be stored on one tiny memory card. After fifty years of using film I have finally been convinced to modernise and am now the proud owner of a Nikon digital SLR.

Another big bonus of this modern technology is the ease with which prints can be made. No longer is it necessary to lock yourself away in a stuffy darkroom surrounded by dishes of smelly chemicals.

The well-known haulier, Lloyds of Ludlow, ceased operations only this year. When this S-registered Volvo F10 was photographed at Toddington Services in June 1979 the company was at its height and running regular services to Europe.

Eight-wheeled flats and dropsiders were already becoming rarities by the mid-'seventies as artics dominated the UK haulage scene. Crane Pumps had this impressive Seddon Atkinson 400 new in 1978 and it is seen at the dealers, Scotts of Bedford when fairly new.

Swedish trucks were all-round pace setters. Like Volvo, Scanias were well liked by drivers. While the LB110 was the top of the range motor, the less powerful LB80 also took the UK market by storm. This one, seen near Victoria, London in March 1976, belonged to CT Transport of Castleford, West Yorks.

The hit and miss nature of 'wet' processing can also be quite wasteful. Having to allow drying time and having to mix up fresh developer and fixer adds to the drudgery.

Of course, not having a physical negative or transparency can be a bit disconcerting when you've been used to the old fashioned system for so long. What would happen if the digital image were accidentally deleted? With a negative you can always go back to it and work from the original but if you lose a computer image there's nothing left. A

back-up CD is the best answer. One great advantage of digital imaging is that you don't lose quality in copying.

With cameras, as with many other things, 'you gets what you pays for' and to get good results you need a reasonably good camera. Cameras have improved immensely since the 'fifties, especially in terms of automated settings, and are proportionately more affordable. If only such equipment had been available when I started, some of my early efforts would have been lot more successful!

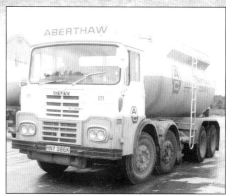

Short wheelbase eight-wheeled bulk tankers have always appealed to me. They look so well balanced and purposeful. This 1972 Guy Big J8 was photographed in 1979 at the Aberthaw Cement Works near Rhoose in South Wales.

The Bedford KM six-wheeler seen here is dwarfed by its big sister – a Detroit Diesel 8V71-powered TM3800 belonging to M&R Transport of Thurleigh, Beds. The TM is seen tipping a load of wheat at the docks in Lowestoft in November 1977.

The docks at Lowestoft provide the setting for this smart 1977 registered Leyland Buffalo artic in the livery of Grantham Road Services. This was towards to end of the fixed-head 500 era. The troublesome 'headless wonder' gave way to the TL11 in the Buffalo 2. Leyland also offered the Buffalo with the naturally aspirated L12.

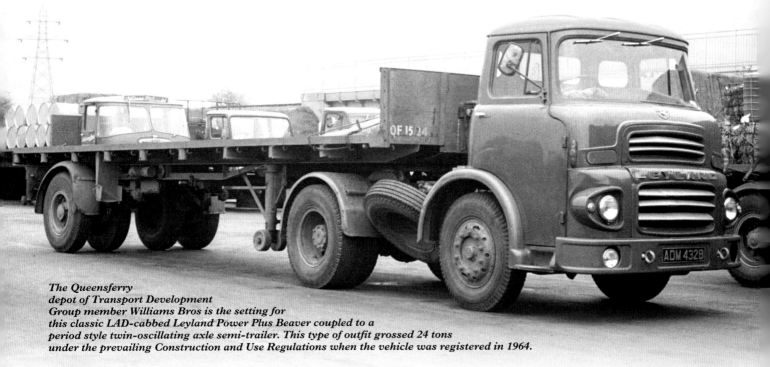

The Queensferry
depot of Transport Development
Group member Williams Bros is the setting for
this classic LAD-cabbed Leyland Power Plus Beaver coupled to a
period style twin-oscillating axle semi-trailer. This type of outfit grossed 24 tons
under the prevailing Construction and Use Regulations when the vehicle was registered in 1964.

CONFESSIONS OF A TRUCK PHOTOGRAPHER

PART 8

Peter Davies concludes the story of his 50 years of photography with a look some of the things that went wrong!

People sometimes come up to me at rallies and say: "I bet you're in your element here with all these old lorries to photograph". The short answer to that is: "No, I'm not!" I explain that it's modern lorries that appeal to me most and that has always been the case. I just can't get enthusiastic about restored lorries unless they are turned out to look like normal working lorries.

Though not the best of pictures technically speaking, this hastily grabbed shot of a Bedford TJ dropside truck belonging to Tuckwell Builders' Merchants is in a nice setting along the old A40 trunk road.

True, there are some excellent examples of properly restored lorries, but the majority are nothing more than sterile showpieces that do absolutely nothing for me. Modern ERF ECTs, Foden Alpha A3-8Rs and Scania R470s do a lot more.

Of course, taking pictures at rallies is safe and acceptable and you don't have to deal with aggression from suspicious drivers. Sadly there will always be the occasional confrontation when drivers get the wrong end of the stick, but, thankfully, it doesn't happen very often. Years go by without such incidents but the risk is never far away.

It's quite extraordinary the effect a camera has on some people. I have been subjected to vicious verbal attacks and even threatened with violence by drivers who get the wrong idea.

Such an incident took place some years ago at a motorway service area. I spotted this nice Scania eight-wheeler in the livery of Tarmac Topblock and, just as I was about to take a shot, the bloke in the lorry next to it (a somewhat boring box van from an own account fleet) leapt out of his cab and rushed towards me hurling abuse.

DAF 2600s were nowhere near as common as their 2800 successors, so I was pleased to capture this example at Toddington Services in April 1975. Renwicks Freight was a big organisation at that time, having taken over several high profile hauliers, including William Nuttall of Manchester, Viney's of Bruton, Arthur Wood of Salford, Edwards of Lydbrook and GC Morley of Bradford.

"What the f*** are you doing with that camera?" he shouted. He then went on to threaten me with GBH and to smash my camera if I dared take a picture. I pointed out to him that I wasn't photographing his lorry but the one next to it. This did nothing to calm his frenzy. I suggested that if he wanted to settle things why not get the police.

He replied, "Never mind the f***ing police - when I've finished with you, you'll need a f***ing ambulance!". All this from a complete stranger who hadn't a clue what the transport hobby is all about. Having strained his brain cell to the limit with all his ranting and raving, he deliberately stood in my way, determined to prevent me from getting a shot of the Scania. How sad is that?

There have been other occasions when self-appointed guardians of the trucking fraternity have popped up at inopportune moments. Once I was about to take a shot of a smart ERF C series artic bulk powder tanker at a services when this singularly obnoxious woman intervened, claiming that she was "Star Lady" and that I was not going to photograph this truck if she had anything to do with it.

She banged on the cab door of the ERF and told the somewhat bemused driver not to worry as she was going to stop me taking a picture. "Where's your bar, mate" she says. "What bar?" asks the driver. "You know", says Star Lady, "drivers always have an iron bar in their cabs. Let me borrow it and I'll sort him out for you." She was all of twenty stone and built like a brick outhouse so I began to wonder who would fare the worst in the impending fracas.

Purely by coincidence a police car came along. I flagged him down and pointed out to the officer that there was a woman threatening to attack me. He told me that they'd had trouble with her before but she wasn't quite bad enough to be locked up. I'm glad to say that was the only encounter I had with Star Lady - oh, and I never got the picture!

This is the last episode in my eight-part series on truck photography but my enthusiasm for recording the haulage scene is as great as ever. No doubt there are many drivers still puzzled by my periodic appearances at the roadside, armed with

The York Trailer Co had a rather exotic taste in tractors during the Sixties. Its fleet which, at that time, ran on general trade plates, included such rarities as a Steyr 91 Series, a "flat face" Kenworth K Series and this DAF T1800, sometimes nicknamed the "Coalscuttle" DAF. The picture dates from November 1966.

Posing in the bright evening sunshine in June 1967 at Lea Road lorry park, Luton, this Atkinson Mk I Silver Knight of Isaac Caswell was loaded with baled steel scrap and awaiting the night man to head off back to South Wales.

It's always nice to get a bit of action into a photograph and this scene has it all. It shows a 1972 Leyland Bison mixer delivering to a building site in Luton in May 1974. Mixconcrete had a plant opposite the Blue Circle Cement Works at Houghton Regis, Beds.

Forerunner of the highly popular Scania LB80 was the fixed-cab Scania Vabis LB76. Now much sought after classics, they were never as common as the later models. This nicely sheeted artic of Waverley Transport was photographed at Toddington Services in September 1975.

my new Nikon. "What's he up to," they probably wonder. Drivers in the Fifties probably wondered the same. Today's pictures, like those from 50 years ago, will in the future be precious snapshots of transport history.

What began as a personal and rather lonely hobby back in the Fifties became a lifelong pursuit and, more recently, a small business venture. After storing all those pictures away for years I have decided to market selected images in the form of photo CDs which enthusiasts can view on their PCs or on most modern DVD players. The colour and black and white images recall bygone scenes and bring to life many of the old classic trucks that can now be seen only at rallies. Available CDs are listed on my website www.pdtruckphotos.com.

Many of the grand Victorian warehouses that graced Liverpool's waterfront were demolished during the Seventies, robbing the city of its unique atmosphere and history. This nicely liveried AEC Mandator artic of Chris Metcalfe, Keighley, is seen passing one of the few precious surviving warehouses along the dock road in October 1978.

Seddon Atkinson was still a new kid on the block when this T36R265 artic tipper entered the Hall and Co fleet in 1976. Note the use of super singles on the trailer axles. These not only saved weight but also reduced the risk of debris being thrown up from dual wheels. The outfit was photographed near Kingston-on-Thames in June 1980.

Robson's Border Transport made Flitwick, Beds, its main southern base in the Eighties, after its takeover by United Glass. Living just a few minutes walk away from such a nice fleet was an enthusiast's dream. Sadly the company, having become part of NYK Shipping and changed its name to UCI Logistics, and moved to a new business park at nearby Marston about 2000, but not before I had captured many of its trucks on camera!

Rallygoers may well recognise this ERF 66TSGX3 "Chinese six" as it was eventually rescued for preservation. 302TD is seen here in February 1987 when it was still working in the fleet of oil engine manufacturers Norris Henty and Gardners, Patricroft, Lancs.

Above: Rounding off the series with a shot taken on my new Nikon digital SLR seems appropriate. This superb Scania R470 artic of A and E Transport, Sheffield, was photographed on the M1 at Toddington just a couple of weeks ago.

Left: Clear sunshine, blue skies and a bright red truck - perhaps the best formula for a cracking shot! Ken Elsby's new Foden S106T was just asking to be snapped at Toddington Services in April 1984. It was among the first of the new Paccar-inspired 6x4s to enter service.

FODEN DEBUTANTE

Not many restorers can claim have to have won a top award with their first project. Nick Larkin visits father and son Derek and Garry Fox to find out more about their 1944 Foden DG - and future projects.
(Photo: Nick Larkin)

Superb first restoration - this 1944 Foden DG was a deserved star at Gaydon.

Cunning restorers? Fox family logo.

Every weekend I was racing around and blowing up engines. It just didn't matter if anything got damaged though.

Pardon? Not quite the words we'd expect from half the restoration duo which has just won arguably the classic commercial movement's most coveted award. Hope we've not gone round to the wrong house!

Fortunately, Garry Fox explains: "My hobby's always been stock car racing until now." Phew. Garry has won many cups over the past 15 years or so, but we can

safely predict that the trophy shelf will be bowing with the weight of classic commercial awards before long.

Anyone who attended the 2005 Classic Commercial Motor Show will have been surprised by the superb 1944 Foden DG 6/12 restored by Garry and his dad Derek. Rather less surprisingly, it was voted best in show and top 1941-50 vehicle. A major achievement in itself, but even more so considering this lorry is their first restoration. And what's more, the Lancashire duo have built up a collection of further projects, and work has started.

Garry reckons his stock car career has helped him to develop the skills to tackle

Keruing used for floor of flat.

The family firm!

the rather contrasting Foden. "I developed metalwork and mechanical skills from building my own cars and repairing the engines when they blew up." Now that is skill.

So why the transition into lorries? "We've always loved Fodens," Garry explained. "I thought it would be good to restore one, just to show my dad what I could do. Now we have half a dozen between us."

Garry and Derek run timber merchants Derek Fox and Sons, set up in 1965 at Ribchester, near Preston, before moving to Longridge. Further premises, including a sawmill, were taken over at Withnell in 2000.

"Part of the reason I think is because the first HGV I drove was a Foden. We had a Foden with a Gardner. It's the wagon I remember my dad and I could hold a conversation in. I wanted an S39 originally as those are what I always remember. Every second wagon seemed to be one at one stage - there were all those Robsons of Carlisle ones for example."

Derek had different ideas. "I always loved the shape of the DG cab, surely the best looking lorry of all time."

Garry then heard of an example being available. LOA 203 was first registered on December 21, 1944, to the Military, then passing to Lucas Batteries, who must have been responsible for the Birmingham 'civvy' registration.

Along with another Lucas DG LOA 203 was eventually sold to Harry Sutton, a showman in Ross-on-Wye. Both vehicles then passed to George Scarrett, from Wootton Bassett, near Swindon, Wilts, but the sister vehicle was written off in the mid 60s.

LOA soldiered on until 1975-6. This extremely rare six-wheeler was then parked in a field until bought by an enthusiast who stripped it down to make a start. He may have found it a daunting task, and Garry bought the lorry in August 2002.

Back in Lancashire, Garry's first thought was "wondering what I'd done - my dad said I was crackers."

Worm axles rebuilt - no easy task.

Foden shakes some dust in woodyard!

Lots of polished wood (mostly original!) in cab.

Lucky mascot - 1944 farthing!

But Derek really thought differently. He came back from a three-month holiday and as Garry says: "That was it. He was at the restoration every minute."

"I got carried away," quips Derek. Mark Roskell who works for the Foxs, also did a lot of work on the lorry.

Garry added: "It certainly couldn't have been restored without both of them. The thing was though that Dad would often ask me to give me a hand with something for a minute and that minute would last two hours."

The lorry, already stripped down, was reduced to its chassis rails, which were shotblasted, as were the wheels.

"We've had every nut and bolt off, gone right through it - new brake cylinders, everything. Shoes, drums, the lot," Garry revealed.

It was obvious that parts were going to be difficult to find. "Being a 1944 vehicle there aren't many spares around but we managed to get the remains of a DG eight-wheeler which was scrap, but had some useful things on it particularly the cab. The one on LOA was in a state but we were able to build it up using parts from the donor.

Reframing was carried in ash, a new plywood skin also being fitted on the rear panel. "We wanted the cab to look like that of a working vehicle," explained Derek, who did most of the work here, including the coachpainting, assisted by wife Stella.

The Gardner 6LW engine was generally in good order but was stripped down, fitted with new rings and the valves reseated. "It definitely needed de-sludging as well," recalled Garry.

Rebuilding the fuel pump and injectors was entrusted to specialist George Gordon, of Longridge. "He was so pleased to be working on a Gardner again instead of all these electronic modern pumps," recalled Derek.

The gearbox was dismantled and teeth were found to be missing on one of the gears. A replacement gear came from a donor box.

All three axles were stripped and rebuilt. Garry recalls: "They're worm drive and I

Foden as found in field (restoration photos courtesy Garry and Derek Fox).

Cab more or less complete but not a pretty sight.

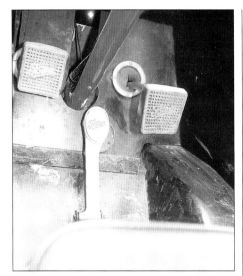

Foden has a centre throttle - that's the brake where you'd expect the accelerator to be.

Note the military style trio of filter bowls. Lorry will top 20mph top speed by the way!

Foden DG cab - the best looker of all time, reckons Derek Fox.

was told not to mess with them. The front one had a hell of a lot of lash in it so I talked to the experts who gave me a few points on how to do it. I set them up and I was told that if they didn't get warm in the first half mile of driving they'd be perfect. They've never been warm yet so I must have set them right."

Foden specialists John Sanderson and Malcolm Sample helped with various spares, and Garry and Derek advertised for others.

A 2in master cylinder was among the difficult finds. Garry rebuilt the Hydrovac, putting new leather seals in it.

The original radiator was rebuilt, Derek having the unenviable task of straightening the fins on the radiator tubes.

As a military vehicle, the Foden was supplied new with two fuel tanks, but the Foxs decided to make do with one, an exchange unit from John Sanderson. The three fuel filter bowls remain on the chassis though.

Next big task was the new body, the flat being constructed in keruing, the bearers and side raves being made from other hardwood. New rear wings were built up by Garry.

Rewiring was the work of renowned electrician and lorry restorer Trevor Barlow. Headlights came from the family of Lionel Amos in Gloucester.

Signwriting was carried out by specialist Tim Eaves, providing a fine finishing touch.

Garry treated me to a quick run around the block in the Foden, and quiet it is not, but well put together it certainly is. The brakes are excellent too!

As we've said, the Foden has surprised everyone who's seen it with the quality of this first time restoration and its workmanlike appearance. "We could definitely get a day's work from it, though of course we'd have to tax it first."

So were the duo surprised by their big rally win? "We'd never had it judged before, so it we didn't know what to expect," recalled Garry.

On the subject of surprises, you probably won't need smelling salts on learning that this father and son team are cracking on with their second restoration, another DG. There's also a further example on the waiting list, along with a delicious FE two-stroke and an S20, plus an S108 which the Foxs operated until a couple of years ago.

We can safely look forward to more star restorations from this stable it seems!

Gardner engine not in bad condition but needed desludging.

They said it was a total stripdown - here are the chassis rails.

Coming together with new flat framing and wings in place.

CEMENTING ATTRACTION

After 30 years lying in the undergrowth, this wonderful 1957 Foden FG6/15 has been restored to its original Blue Circle Cement specification. In the first of two articles, Peter Davies describes the lorry's rescue and dismantling.
(Photos: Peter Davies)

Magnificent - grey industrial setting shows off the bright yellow on 1957 Blue Circle Foden FG6/15.

Foden owner and restorer Gary Baker

One of the of the best known lorry fleets of all was that of the Cement Marketing Co, with its Blue Circle trademark. Like other own account operators such as Tate and Lyle and Rank, the CMC was a major Foden user in the Fifties and Sixties. A number of the firm's vehicles have survived but until now no one has taken the trouble to return any of them to original Blue Circle livery. That wrong has now been righted by dedicated Foden enthusiast Gary Baker.

Gary, 56, has held a lifelong interest in Foden lorries - his dad drove eight-wheelers for a living. Gary's earlier restoration projects included a superb S20 eight-wheeler in Elliott's of Bournemouth livery. Anyone who has Harold Nancollis's excellent book on Foden will have seen Gary's S20, The Emperor, on the cover.

The first thing that strikes you about his latest restoration, this 1957 FG6/15, is the astonishing degree of accuracy in the livery and signwriting. Even such details as the characteristic First Aid Kit sign and similar notices in the cab interior are reproduced in detail. Looking at the lorry you would think it had just been supplied new to the Cement Marketing Co, ready to enter service.

Not much is known about the Foden's working history, though it's believed to have operated from the Gateshead area. It was new as fleet number 1350, one of a pair of vehicles (the sister, 1349, being registered SXY 260) with a dual-purpose tipper body. This meant the lorry could be used as a flat to transport bagged cement, or, by fitting a sealed cover, could carry bulk loads. When the lorry was new, bulk hauling of cement was in its infancy, as most customers just took cement in bags which they'd store in sheds. At one point, having the product as a single bulk load would give them a 20 per cent a ton discount.

It was probably the unusual body which meant the Foden was sold out of service for scrap in the late 1960s rather than beginning a new career with

Here's how CVC reported the Foden's rescue - back in our September 1998 issue.

showmen etc.

Luckily, the Foden, or at least most of it, survived, though the first class results of all Gary's hard work give no hint of the vehicle's appalling condition when it was hauled out of the undergrowth where it had lain for over 30 years. This was no job for the faint-hearted. Only an enthusiast as dedicated as Gary would have attempted it.

Despite the alloy cab and tipping body being almost intact and in surprisingly good shape, the lorry was lacking many vital components, not least its Gardner

6LW engine and Foden gearbox. The radiator and front crossmember were also missing.

Needless to say, after such a long time at the mercy of the elements, the condition of the chassis and running gear was such that a complete strip down and rebuild was required. This was a nut and bolt restoration in the real sense and it took Gary and his many supportive friends seven long years to complete.

Gary's son Benjamin was just 10 years old when TLD was first rescued for

preservation. He is now 17 and, like his dad, is a keen Foden fan and played a useful role in helping with the restoration.

To tell the full story we must go back to 1992, when Gary first set eyes on the Foden during a visit to that wellknown shrine of classic trucks, Rush Green Motors of Langley, near Stevenage, Herts.

It looked very tempting and Gary could picture the forlorn FG in all its splendour when it was still working back in the Sixties. As is often the case, negotiations with dealers can go on for some time - six years in this instance, but eventually an agreement was reached and TLD 778 was Gary's.

Next job was to get it home - no easy task! Just extricating it from its resting place was a challenge in itself but the team at Rush Green Motors take such things in their stride. On June 26, 1998, the Foden was to move for the first time in over three decades, even if it was with the help of a crane.

Another one-time Foden aficionado, Charles Roads from Willingham, Cambridge, came to the party with his trusty Atkinson Borderer hitched to a low-loader. Gary ensured that the whole procedure was well recorded on camera.

Convertible body was specially built to carry sacks of cement or bulk loads.

Soon TLD was being whisked away along the M4 bound for its new home in Weston-super-Mare, Somerset. Gary couldn't wait to get weaving on the restoration. First, though, there was the matter of a visit to the Foden Gathering at Banbury the following day. It was decided to put the Foden on display in as found condition and it was there I saw it for the first time since I had enthused over it many years earlier at Rush Green.

CVC readers might recall Gary's story As Found, which I wrote for the September 1998 issue. In it Gary was quoted as saying that TLD 778 would be returned to its original livery and, sure enough, he has been true to his word.

Once the lorry was back at Weston, Gary wasted no time in stripping it down. The cab was lifted off in October 1998 and a couple of months later it was shotblasted. Considering it had been exposed to the elements for over three decades it was in surprisingly good shape, thanks largely to its all-alloy construction.

Only the front panels needed replacing plus a grille panel, as the original had gone missing. Once all the grime and old paint was off, the cab was given a protective coat of primer and the interior was sprayed with two-pack paint in light brown to match the original finish.

The Redhill light alloy cab, built by Redhill Bodybuilding Industries, Crawley, Sussex, is a design more-or-less exclusive to the Cement Marketing Co. While the grille and front panel are identical with the standard S18, the rest of the cab differs. The windscreen is more upright and the centre pillar is wider. The interior is much more spartan, having all-metal framework and no lining or insulation. However, one real advantage of the Redhill cab over the standard S18 is that there is no timber to rot away. Anyone who has tackled the restoration of an S18 cab has faced a daunting carpentry job.

Although the Gardner 6LW and the original five-speed Foden gearbox were missing, Gary was able to locate suitable replacements thanks to John Sanderson, at Smallwood, Cheshire, who is well known as a source of all things Foden.

One small deviation from TLD's original specification has been the fitting of a 12-speed gearbox. This does not affect the appearance of the lorry but it

Cab, built by Redhill, was more or less exclusive to the Cement Marketing Co.

Blue Circle became a household name.

TLD 778 as found at Rush Green Motors. This is where she stood for 30 years.

Body being craned off at Westbury Cement Works, March 4, 1999.

Bare chassis in the workshop at Westbury, March 4, 1999.

Crane moves in on June 26, 1998, to begin extracting the Foden.

Moving the Foden into position ready to load on to Charles Roads' Atkinson.

Chassis strip down begins, April 9, 1999.

The tricky job of getting loading the Foden on to the low-loader.

Arrival at Greenaways Farm, near Kewstoke, Somerset, June 29, 1998.

Chassis sidemembers awaiting re-assembly, April 1999

Cab removed October 1998.

Cab being shotblasted, December 8, 1998.

This pile of bits illustrates the extent Gary went to in dismantling the Foden

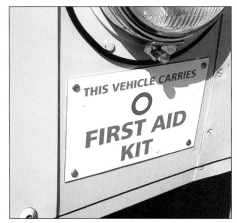

Authenticity stretches to 'first aid' sign.

enables it to gain a bit more road speed - important if you're taking it out in today's traffic. The engine needed an extensive overhaul, a job entrusted to Gardner experts Watts, of Lydney, Glous. Dave Barlow rebuilt the engine after Watts carried out a number of repairs including honing the liners.

At first the lorry was housed at a farm in Kewstoke, but the staff at the Westbury works of Lafarge Cement, which now owns Blue Circle, were very enthusiastic about the project and provided workshop space, which was a great boon to Gary.

"The lads at Westbury, Glenn, Richie and Geoff, were good enough to put up with me for at least two years and I thank them sincerely for all the support

they gave me, Gary told me. He added: "I also owe a lot of gratitude to the late Brian Scott, who was workshop manager but sadly passed away last year. Without his help and all the other help I had at Westbury, the project would have been a great deal harder".

Removing the heavy tipping body was quite a task in itself and the lads at Westbury came to the rescue with a mobile crane. Gradually, bit-by-bit, over the coming months TLD was dismantled down to the last nut and

bolt. Each component was cleaned and painted or replaced where necessary. It was a painstaking process that was going to take Gary another six years.

NEXT MONTH
In part two we'll report further on how the restoration took shape and how the Foden was transformed into the magnificent machine it is today.

With the sealed cover shown here, the truck became a bulk carrier.

CEMENTING – PART 2

This magnificent 1957 Foden FG6/15 has been restored to the highest standards after 30 years lying in the undergrowth. In this second part of the restoration story, we see how restorer Gary Baker put the vehicle back together. Peter Davies reports. (Photos: Peter Davies)

By April 1999, just 10 months after this 1957 Foden FG6/15 was pulled out of the undergrowth at Rush Green Motors, in Hertfordshire, two chassis sidemembers lay on pallets awaiting re-assembly. At this stage all the crossmembers, spring hangers, etc. had been thoroughly cleaned and repainted. Once the frame was rebuilt, the next stage was to get TLD 778 back on its springs and axles so that the Foden was once more a rolling chassis.

The overhauled 6LW engine was installed during 1999. Progress during the first 12 months had been pretty impressive but there was still a massive amount to do. A thorough check had to be made of every mechanical component, including the braking system, steering and tipping gear. A complete brake rebuild was carried out by Gary's friend and fellow enthusiast Mark Wiltshire. Mark himself owns a restored Foden and a Scania and is a skilled mechanic.

All along the line, Gary received valuable assistance from the workshop staff at Lafarge Cement's Westbury works, and the company was very generous in sponsoring a complete set of new tyres - a big part of the cost when you're working on a limited budget.

Gary was careful to keep an accurate record of all the signwriting and to obtain colour samples to match the original Blue Circle Yellow and Oxford Blue. The chassis and the cab roof on TLD were finished in Light Aircraft Grey. The old signwriting had, remarkably, survived quite well and this was traced so that it could be reproduced exactly as original.

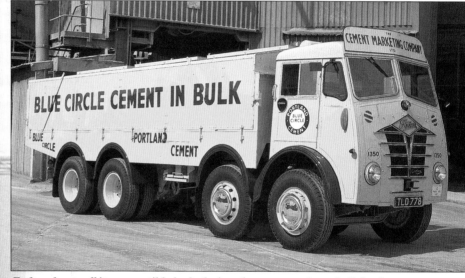

Foden shows off its convertible body designed to carry sacks or bulk loads.

Left: Foden restored to absolutely authentic condition.

Foden squares up to modern DAF: Lafarge, a French company, now owns the Blue Circle brand name.

Up she rises! Tipper body had survived intact during Foden's long stay at Rush Green Motors.

Tipping gear was reconditioned.

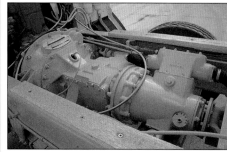

A 12-speed gearbox has been fitted to help Foden cope with modern traffic conditions.

Below: Looking absolutely at home in cement works!

Having got the chassis/cab back into a more or less complete state, it was time to tackle the bodywork. TLD 778, fleet no 1350, was one of a small number of special dual-purpose lorries operated by the Cement Marketing Co. Its sister vehicle was SXY260, fleet no 1349. They entered service at a time when bulk delivery was still a relatively new service. Many customers still required bagged cement, so the Cement Marketing Co, as well as the other major cement manufacturers, needed lorries that could be adapted to either type of delivery.

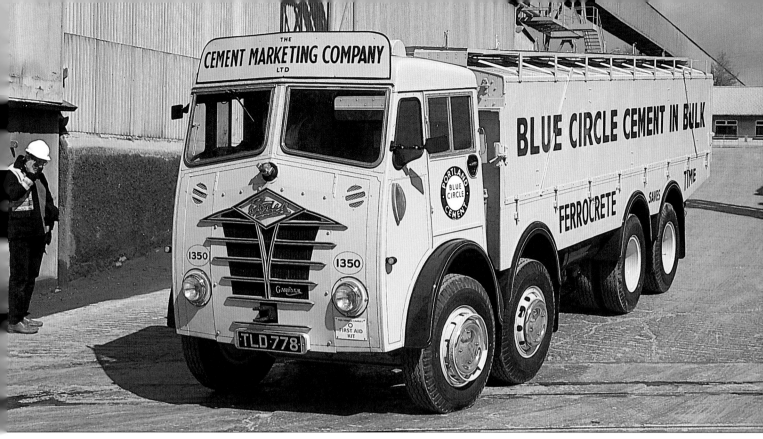

TLD has a platform body built by G Scammell and Nephew to the CMC's own design. However, it also has tipping rams and a removable bulk cover, so that it can deliver bulk as well as bags. The body is 22ft long - some 4ft longer than the average tipping body and, for a tipper, has a longer than usual rear overhang. Fleet numbers 1349 and 1350 are believed to be

the only two such vehicles with S18 cabs but some similar dual-purpose lorries were built about the same time with S20 cabs.

Although complete, the old body needed extensive repairs and it was decided to replace the side skirts and the side panels on the bulk cover. This work was carried out by local bodybuilding and engineering specialist Julian Hobbs and

his staff. It was all done to original specification and the result is spot-on.

By 2000, the body had been replaced on the chassis and the tipping gear was working perfectly. From then on all the cosmetic work had to be completed. The restoration was far from over - there was still an enormous amount to do. Jobs included fitting out the cab and replacing

Signwriting absolutely authentic. Enough of the original had survived for it to be traced.

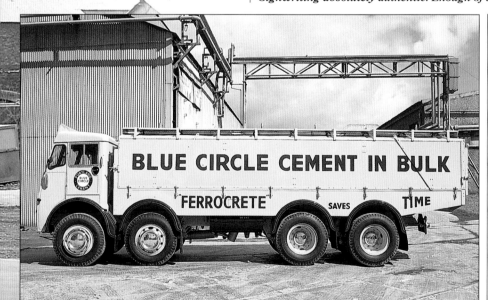

The 22ft long body was anything but standard and the tipping gear made it heavy - probably why the Foden didn't have a second in service life after leaving CMC.

Brightwork beautifully restored.

53

GARY'S TIPS FOR RESTORERS

- Stay in touch with friends who have specialist skills so that advice and assistance is there when you want it.
- Don't do things by halves. If a job's worth doing it's worth doing properly.
- Only buy a vehicle that you're really keen on so that you don't lose interest in the project.
- Here's the best tip of all - don't buy a project in the first place!

This official shot of sister vehicle SXY 260 was a useful reference point during the restoration.

The rebuilt 6LW is installed in the chassis later in 1999.

Though complete, the body underwent extensive re-panelling in July 2000.

Worm's-eye-view of the newly repainted rear bogie.

January 2002 - Gary poses with the rebuilt chassis/cab.

By late 2002 the Foden could be driven about the yard.

Almost there - but there was still a lot of detail finishing work to do.

Correct spec replacement Gardner 6LW engine sourced. The original had been removed.

Seats look brand new 1950s spec.

the glazing, fitting new wings and all the hundred and one details such as beading and so on. A full rewire was of course required and all the lights had to be replaced.

Gradually all the tedious finishing work was completed and the time came to carry out the finished paint job and to signwrite the Foden back into full period Blue Circle livery.

The paint job was completed by Wayne at CRT Auto Bodies, Weston-super-Mare, Somerset. "He did a fantastic job", says Gary. Signwriting was entrusted to Colin Ford, who reproduced the original livery with meticulous accuracy. By studying photos of the vehicle as found and of its sister vehicle, fleet no 1349, Colin was able to ensure that all the lettering was correctly positioned to match that on TLD when she was in service.

Gary was careful to see that all the other details, such as Foden's distinctive step rings and external fittings, were exactly right. Similarly, the number plates, something often overlooked by restorers, are of the exact size and specification and are correctly positioned. A common mistake is to hang the front number plate below the cab panel - something you never saw on Fodens. All in all the restored lorry is as close to original as possible and is a credit to Gary and his many helpers.

As a keen enthusiast of Cement Marketing Co vehicles I am personally thrilled to finally see one done up properly, having bemoaned the fact that none of the surviving examples have so far been correctly restored. TLD 778 is a shining example of just how a lorry should be restored and Gary can feel justly proud of what he has achieved.

For our photo shoot we were kindly allowed to take the Foden to Lafarge Cement's Aberthaw Works in South

Cab restoration absolutely accurate.

Wales, where it could be posed in its true working environment. This was arranged by John Capewell, Works Manager at Lafarge's Hope Works in Derbyshire. John has taken a close interest in Gary's restoration and is a keen vehicle enthusiast himself, his speciality being Range Rovers.

It wasn't the first time Gary's Foden had been seen in public - it was put on display in partly-restored form at an open day at Hope Works in September 2003 after John came to hear about the project.

When moving the Foden about Gary is indebted to Towers WSM for the loan of their low-loader.

There's more good news in the offing. Now that TLD is complete, Gary has already started work on an even more demanding project. Lurking in his shed is a 1946 Foden DG6/15 which has come off the fairgrounds. It has been much modified and has an S18 cab. There are plans to put the DG back to standard form and to finish it in a wellknown haulage livery. Enough said: if the result is anything like as good as TLD then we're all going to be in for a treat when it's done.

Gary extends his heartfelt thanks to all those who have helped him with the restoration of TLD 778, not least Lafarge Cement, which has shown a great deal of interest in the project. "One other thing," says Gary. "I would like to thank my wife Caroline for putting up with me spending every weekend working on the lorry!"

CIRCLE LIN

(Photos: Glyn Barney)

A stunning newcomer to this year's rally scene has been an ex-Blue Circle Cement Scammell Routeman owned by Dave Pearson, a driver with the company. We take the beast back to its original depot, hear the full restoration story, and discover another Scammell waiting in the wings!

Nick Larkin reports.

Blue Circle Cement

SCAMMELL

2052H

JYM 149W

Blu
Ce.

WC TANKER GROUP LTD

t's easy to understand why a rock band, fashion model or soap powder has become a household name. But a cement company? Mention Blue Circle to anyone and they'll chirp the word 'cement' back at you. And even someone whose hobby is flower arranging rather than classic lorries would probably recognise a member of Blue Circle's vivid yellow transport fleet.

Not surprising, then, that one of this year's newcomers to the commercial vehicle rally scene has attracted more attention from Mr and Mrs Public than just about anything else.

ES!

A return to a silo where it often loaded. The silos are loaded from underground, by the way, the cement being blown up into them.

Blue Circle Cement

WG TANKER GROUP LTD

Ram, made by Drum, was in good condition.

Back where it used to be! Scammell Routeman at Blue Circle's Cauldon Works in Staffordshire.

Blue Circle Cement

SCAMMELL

Scammell at Cauldon. Blue Circle contributed towards the restoration.

57

Scammell was found in use as a test bed unit on loan to Drum Engineering.

Scammell on tow back to its new owner's base. A subsequent test drive showed it was by no means roadworthy!

Tanker body takes about two minutes to raise fully.

It could be 1981 again. Scammell roars away f. Cauldon weighbridge.

Dave Pearson's 1981 Scammell Routeman tanker has already taken several awards, but its real accolade is its ability to turn the heads of those whose minds are more likely to be concentrated on whether or not to have fish fingers for tea. Any high street it rumbles through, any retail park it roars past, and people will look.

The rich note of the Leyland TL11 engine also adds to the mixture of course, as does the fact that the vehicle is immaculately clean. Certainly the unmistakable cab design, wonderfully executed by legendary stylist Michelotti, plays a large part. First, it looks like nothing else, so there's more than a hint of nostalgic recognition, especially around the area in which the Scammell was based.

Secondly – well this is my theory anyway – the cab doesn't have the wide front grille in chrome/black etc as seen on today's vehicles. So it's uncompromisingly yellow. A banana seems blue by comparison. Put this Scammell by its modern equivalent and it doesn't look incredibly dated, just so much more stylish.

Interestingly, plans for this cab go far back as 1961, when Michelotti was working under contract to Leyland. He would design cars such as the Triumph Herald, Spitfire, TR4 and Dolomite. An approach was made to him by Scammell, which had been taken over by Leyland in 1955, and this cab was the result. It was unveiled at the 1962 Motor Show and was used on the Routeman and eventually a variety of other Scammells.

58

Scammell chassis was in superb condition. Here it is being shotblasted.

Ribbing looks impressive but is a nightmare to paint.

Owner Dave Pearson with the Scammell and his modern steed, a DAF

Blue Circle has a long history, the name being created in 1920. The concern actually goes back to the Associated Portland Cement Manufacturers (1900) Ltd. Though today Blue Circle is involved with a diverse range of industry, it will forever be famous for the cement side of the business.

Fleetwise, Foden had been Blue Circle's main supplier for more than 30 years until 1970, when the firm turned its attention to Scammell. By 1977, 750 Routeman were in service, Blue Circle preferring rigids rather than artics, not least because the vehicles would spend much of their time on the often uncertain terrain of quarries and building sites.

Dave Pearson's Scammell, JYW 149W, was among the last batch of 20 Routeman delivered to Blue Circle. Powered by a turbocharged TL11 turbo engine, as fitted to the last 45 Routeman, the Blue Circle examples ran at 30 ton gross.

Dave's vehicle has a six-speed AEC gearbox. The tanker body was made by Metalair, a Blue Circle subsidiary, and has a 20-ton capacity, the Scammell being 30 ton gross.

The vehicle was delivered new to the Blue Circle cement works at Cauldon, Staffs, being based there throughout its working life. It had fleetnumber 2052H, the letter referring to the batch, not the depot.

Dave explains why the Scammell has a London, rather than Staffordshire, registration. "All vehicles at that time were distributed from Blue Circle's central handling workshops Beddington, near Wimbledon. It would have gone there as a chassis and would have the tanks, blowers and mudguards fitted to Blue Circle specification."

The Beddington workshops were in action for more than 50 years and even built the discharge system at the rear of the tanker, which is stamped "Beddington".

JYW 149W remained in service until 1989, in the hands of one driver, Albert Clear. It was then dispatched to Drum Engineering of Bradford, who had it on loan at their development shop for developing new discharge blowers, which are used to discharge the cement from Scammell to silo.

Dave started work at Blue Circle, Cauldon, 10 years ago, though he's been driving lorries since 1969, previously having worked for Shirley's Transport, Stoke-on-Trent, Tideswells at Kingsley, and the now

Discharge unit was made at Blue Circle's Beddington works.

Scammell styling extended to the door trims.

defunct printers and dyers, Thomas, Arthur Wardle of Leek.

"The Scammells had all gone by the time I arrived at Blue Circle. We were on the roadtrains then, but drivers still had fond memories of the Routeman."

Dave, who had always been a Scammell fan, heard about the vehicle being at Drum's Bradford works. "I went there on the Saturday morning, found out where it was, photographed it, and had to have it."

The Scammell was towed back to Dave's Staffordshire base, where he succumbed to the temptation of a short test drive.

"Took us about two or three hours to get the fuel through and it eventually started. I took it for a run up the yard just to try it. By the time I'd done that, four or five air pipes burst, the air packs were leaking and it was a case of parking it up and starting from scratch."

Thankfully, the engine and turbo were in excellent condition. The brakes were stripped, three new chambers being needed, and all the air pipes were replaced with plastic units, as seen on modern vehicles. The wheels were removed, the chassis was shotblasted and painted. The fibreglass cab had remained in reasonable condition, though some minor filling was needed.

The tanker body had survived well, but new outlet pipes were needed – the discharge unit actually being made at the Blue Circle workshops and carrying the description "Beddington".

The tipping mechanism worked well; it takes about two minutes to fully raise the tank.

As far as loading and unloading is concerned, the tanker is loaded from the top, and when the body is tipped up, the cement goes to the end of the tanker. Air is blown in from the discharge unit at the back and the tanker body acts like a chimney, the cement rising into the silo.

Body repainting was carried out by commercial vehicle painter Mick Davis, from Ashbourne, Derbyshire, using polyurethane paint, a superb job particularly as the Michelotti cab, with its styling ridges, is not the easiest of subjects.

Blue Circle provided much assistance in the restoration, providing the paint and contributing towards the cost of the repaint. The company also found and donated a set of transfers.

"Putting these on a tanker would be a nightmare, and it was best to get professional help here." Dave remembers. Easyfix Emblems of Leek did the job.

WG Tankers of Cauldon, which maintains Blue Circle's tankers,

contributed towards the repaint and provided mudguards. "The originals were plastic with a tin top. I couldn't get any of these anywhere, and so the replacement are steel."

Dave would like to thank both organisations for their assistance, and everyone else who helped with the project. John Ferns, a driver for Blue Circle and expert electrician, tackled the electrics. "Over the years they had left wires here and there, cut wires and made other alterations, but overall the electrics weren't in too bad a condition," recalls Dave.

There was one major problem: "The French Cibie headlights were difficult to get hold of. Apparently they were the same as on a Vauxhall Viva, but they were concave, not convex." Eventually, Lancashire-based Chorley Electrics managed to source a new set of lights.

The interior has worn well, though Dave has just sourced a new headlining.

So after much work and two new tyres being fitted, one immaculate Scammell was ready for action, the result of a two-year project. Its first rally was the 2001 Llandudno event.

"We finally got it finished on the Friday night – Llandudno started on the Saturday. It wasn't even MoT'd until the Friday afternoon." The Scammell

The second Scammell is in surprisingly good condition. It's expected to be restored as a flatbed.

Scammell number 2 in action. It may look like a vehicle from Mad Max, but runs well, although the engine breathes a bit. The exhaust stack was fitted during the vehicle's quarry work era.

Their heyday - Routeman line-up at Cauldon for publicity shot. These earlier vehicles ran at 24 tons gross.

performed admirably on its long journey to Wales, and cruises around 50mph.

The Scammell went on to pick up awards at the CVRTC Gaydon event. So how does Dave sum up the Routeman's appeal? "It's great to drive, the Michelotti styling is superb... and it's a Blue Circle Scammell!"

But Dave's Scammell story doesn't end with JYW 149W. He now has a sister Routeman, minus tanker, registration HYK 612W, fleetnumber 1868X. Another ex-Cauldon vehicle, this machine had spent its latter days as a water bowser on the nearby quarry.

"They'd stopped using it and bought a dumptruck instead. I took pity on it, to be honest. I convinced myself I needed a Scammell for spares, but, considering the time it's spent at the quarry, it's survived well and is even a good runner, though the engine breathes a bit."

Dave's intention is to convert this second Scammell into a flatbed, complete with a

suitable load of cement bags. "They had five of these at Cauldon, and as far as we know, no originals survive."

Talking of survival, you may well be wondering why there are no ex-Blue Circle Scammells around, either on the rally circuit or anywhere else for that matter. There's a simple, if excruciating explanation. Blue Circle was notorious for cutting holes in the tankers and slicing the chassis of its redundant vehicles before scrapping them – so they didn't fall into the hands of competitors.

Today, the Scammells and Leylands are replaced by DAFs, and Cauldon only has some 20 lorries in its fleet. Changes in cement distribution, including a policy of offering discounts to bulk customers who arranged their own collection, meant a rapid reduction in the fleet, which at its peak was around 1600 vehicles and is now less than a quarter of that.

Not all is lost, however. Dave, who also owns a magnificent 1942 Diamond T, has discovered that Blue Circle still has a couple of Scammells used on internal work at another Midlands site. "I've definitely got my eye on those, so watch this space!"

> ★ Many thanks to Blue Circle for allowing us to photograph the Scammell at Cauldon.

Scammell cruises around 50mph on the road.

Here's one we restored earlier...

SIX PA

John Thomas has been responsible for some great restorations over the past decade. Here we feature two of his latest, a 1959 Bedford and 1975 ERF A-series, plus three trailers! We've also just room for a Seddon given a new identity, and some great family archive photos.
(Photos: Nick Larkin)

Take three - Bedford S-type and ERF A-series, plus former BRS Seddon 32/4 now in Ken Thomas Ltd guise.

Bet you've all got your calculators out to make sure we've got the 10 promised restoration stories in the magazine. Well, over the past decade, John Thomas from Cambridgeshire has been responsible for some of the finest restorations we've featured in *CVC*.

Having had a major independent haulage company to run for much of that time, not surprisingly much of the work has been done by top outside specialists, as is the case with that other great collector and restorer based locally, Tony Knowles.

Both however are died-in-the-wool lorry enthusiasts, and on the rare occasions they've been relatively free of time constraints, won't hesitate to wield a spanner.

John had managed to escape a visit from *CVC* for quite a while, so we were delighted to take up an invite to call in.

Especially with our list of 10 restorations hanging over us.

OK, Restoration Counters! Two of our official list are John's latest projects, a 1959 Bedford S-type and a 1975 ERF A-Series.

Looking through our 10 years of issues, we were struck by the fact that we've not really featured many trailer restorations, which, as they do tend to be found behind lorries, might be a bit of an oversight, you may say. So, we're featuring three from John's collection here.

So, there are five out of the 10 here. But, to quote one of the great television

catchphrases of the past decade, "We don't just want to give you that."

We would like to have covered more Seddons, so here's a fine opportunity to catch up with the wellknown former British Road Services 32/4, TCH 615L, recently acquired by John and now presented in the livery of the family firm Ken Thomas Ltd.

As has been well documented, John's father Ken started the business in 1948. He bought the first vehicle for restoration, a 1932 Morris Commercial, in 1966. Many other projects have been added to the list by John, though he once admitted to customising a Ford Transit in the Eighties. John now specialises in self-storage and various other haulage interests.

62

CK

Unfortunate end for Thomas Seddon when it hit a house at Brighouse!
(Photo: John Thomas Collection)

ERF is one of the last A-series built.

THE LORRIES

We'll begin with John's superb 1959 S-type 7-ton tipper, new to a Norfolk farmer who had it for several years. "I understand that in the latter part of its working life it was just used for moving grain etc locally," John told me. He found the vehicle through word of mouth at Melton Constable, Norfolk.

Restoration was completed by the renowned Yorkshire specialist Colin Pitt. A replacement cab was sourced from Norfolk-based Bedford guru John Morter. The cab was powder-blasted and very little welding was found to be needed, though as this was an ex-military type, alterations had to be made to the headlight positions, grilles, etc, to convert it to civvy spec.

The Bedford's body, believed to have been built by Hawson, was stripped and much of the wood was in such good condition that it could be re-used. Some of the steelwork needed welding and repair though!

Mechanically, the Bedford engine didn't need any work apart from an injector overhaul. The brakes were rebuilt and necessary work carried out on the electrics. A respray was carried out in two pack by

Colin Pitt's brother Richard. The seats were reupholstered.

The tipper mechanism was fine apart from the ram needing to be re-sealed, and that was about it. The resulting lorry looks superb, the signwriting, by Andy Moden, of Banner Signs, Wisbech, Cambs, being an especially fine finishing touch.

One slight problem - the Bedford's original plating certificate got lost when it was sent to the DVLA. Luckily, John took

Bedford restored by specialist Colin Pitt, ERF an in-house project.

a photocopy before it went.

The lorry brings back many memories for John of these Bedfords being run by his dad. "He had long wheelbase S-types like this, though dropsides rather than tippers, for use on market work.

"He got good service out of them and then he went to the TK. I remember him always saying that every time Bedford went up a model it did less to the gallon than its predecessor."

Now to the ERF, a P-registered example like several once run in the Thomas fleet. "It was one of the last. Father put some P-registered A-series on the road and some

B-series at the same time," John recalled.

This lorry was run for many years by Norfolk haulier Carter, John buying it at an auction at Mepal last year. "It was a ballast tractor, and had been used for towing a living van."

This restoration would be carried out in-house. One problem though: There was no fifth wheel or mounting plates. It seemed a major fabrication job was going to have be carried out, but then came an incredibly lucky coincidence.

John just happened to be talking to vehicle repainter Norman Smith, who among many other assignments works on

Tony Knowles's lorries. Norman found the ERF's original fifth wheel, mounting plate and run-ups in his yard. "They'd been taken off when he painted the lorry for the previous owner!" John revealed.

Not everything was simple though, as corrosion under the area where the fifth wheel sits had pushed the chassis out.

"We had to take the spring hangers off, all the crossmembers out, all the flitch plates, sandblast and prime it, then thankfully then the fifth wheel bed went straight on."

Otherwise, the chassis and the engine turned out to be in good condition, the

Seddon last seen in BRS guise.

Seddon rebuilt and re-cabbed in Len James's ownership. (Photo: John Thomas Collection)

Bedford cab replaced with converted former military example.

Lots of painted metal in Bedford cab

Good instrumentation in ERF cab.

ERF having been in regular use, though rewiring was needed. An interior back panel in the cab was replaced. Painting was entrusted to Kirk Coachworks, of Guyhirn, Cambs.

John located a correct air cleaner for the Gardner engine, giving the final touch of authenticity.

Despite all this, the ERF didn't have an easy ride at MoT time. "The previous owner had modified all the air valves. It was an absolute nightmare and we had horrendous problems," said John.

And now ... the Seddon 32/4. New to BRS at Melton Mowbray, Leics, this vehicle was originally preserved by John Ward, of Oadby, Leics, and then passed to Len Janes, who had a full restoration carried out by Red Hannon and Colin Pitt in 2001. Kev Dennis located a new cab shell, replacement front grille and a headlamp panel.

New air tanks were made, and a fifth wheel frame fabricated to the pattern of the old one.

A full brake overhaul was carried out, the radiator reconditioned and a new water pump fitted. New injectors were installed and the injector pump overhauled. A new lift pump was needed. The Seddon retains its original Gardner 180 engine and David Brown six-speed gearbox.

Since being acquired by John, the Seddon has been outshopped in Ken Thomas livery and a small amount of work has been carried out to the rear of the chassis.

"The main reason I bought this was that it was a tidy lorry - very tidy - restored more or less to the standards we would do them," said John. Seddons were also operated in the Thomas fleet.

"Father ran two of these, though with Cummins engines. He was a typical British operator. He liked ERFs and he liked Atkinsons and Seddons. Like a lot of operators he wanted Gardner engines."

One of the Thomas Seddons had a rather unfortunate end, in a major accident at Brookfoot Hill near Brighouse, West Yorks, when the driver lost his brakes and hit a house. Thankfully he escaped with only cut knuckles, and no one else was injured.

A solitary S-type remained in Thomas fleet when TKs had taken over! A single Dodge also stands defiantly despite being swamped by TKs. (Photo: John Thomas Collection)

Bedford's tipping mechanism had remained in good condition.

NOW TO THE TRAILERS

Unique surviving Murfitt trailer.

murfitt

platform semis

When did you last see one of these?

First up is a 1971 York, which John was offered by well-known local dealer Joe Fuller, of Chatteris. "He always knows I'm on the look-out for older stuff," said John.

"We stripped the brakes and cleaned them all up, got it MoT-ed, sandblasted and repainted."

A sledge plate, new headboard panel and back crossmember were fitted and the floor was replaced on the 40ft diamond-patterned chassis.

The other two trailers are definitely rarities, the first being of ERF manufacture

and made in the 1960s.

John told me: "In the 1940s and in the 1960s, ERF had a couple of goes at making trailers. I think they sold them as tractor/trailer combinations.

"Apparently there are stories that if you bought ERF tractors and trailers you'd be more likely to get a lorry with a Gardner engine when these were in short supply."

This trailer was operated for many years by Fenmarc Produce, of March, John buying it from Kev Dennis. "As far as I know there are only four or five ERF trailers surviving, and this is the only restored example."

The chassis is partly double skinned.

"The rust got in and split the chassis. We had to cut the rust out of it over a couple of weekends. To be honest I never thought it would go back together."

Keith Wright, who works for John, joined him in this delightful task, which at last was completed. New chuck rails, crossmembers, a back panel and floor were also fitted.

And finally, a possible sole survivor of the trailers made by Murfitt, of Wisbech, who went on to make powder tankers. This one dates from 1969, and was found on a farm at Gedney Hill, Lincs. John swapped two other trailers for it, but he recalls: "When we got it home it was

York 40ft trailer completely rebuilt.

extensively worse than we thought. The chassis was holed all over."

A complete rebuild followed, with new crossmembers, floor and chuck rails needed plus many other parts.

"The interesting thing about this trailer is that whereas crossbearers on most others are punched through the chassis in one piece, on this they are just butted up to the chassis and welded."

Murfitts did appear in the Thomas fleet. "Father ran several. He bought them with

Thomas attention to detail extends to trailers!

single axles which he put behind Commer two-strokes and Ford D-series.

Some were later extended by firms such as Seadyke trailers in Wisbech: "They cut two up to make one and we ran them as 40-footers."

The survivor remains a 29ft 26-tonner, with a York axle. Like several others in the preserved fleet, this one has had to be fitted with rear wings as the original flimsy bits of metal do not comply with modern anti-spray legislation.

Trailers have had to be fitted with new rear wings to comply with modern legislation.

We couldn't resist mentioning another trailer, restored earlier, a 1959 Scammell Fourtrak with Scammell coupling. Another ground-up job, work on this included replacing five or six crossbearers and rebuilding the brakes.

Nothing exactly like this ran in the Thomas fleet, but the firm took over Fenland Transport, of Thorney, near Peterborough, which had some BTC four-in-line ones.

Obviously a lot of superb work has been done here and our congratulations go to John, but what's to come next? "Well, we're hoping to have a Maudslay Mustang finished next, then there's a Bedford TK," he told me.

CVC is definitely looking forward to featuring these - hopefully in the early-ish parts of *CVC*'s second decade!

NUMBERS GAME

So we have the Bedford, and ERF A-series as part of out 10 restorations. The Seddon, which was a major rebuild a few years ago, isn't officially part of the 10, but could have been, but the three trailers are. We've also sneaked in a bit about John's Scammell Fourtrak. Come on, let's settle on the round figure of five restorations here then!

The only known restored ERF trailer.

I f your mustard-coloured Austin Allegro had spluttered to a halt on the M1 in 1975, you'd staggered (in those pre-mobile phone days) for what seemed like miles to a roadside telephone to call the rescue services, and rushed back and waited patiently - you just might have seen the Bedford J2 in this feature before.

The lorry would have looked, and acted rather differently then, however. It would have been bright yellow, for a start, with the letters AA proudly emblazoned on the side.

Out of the vehicle would have stepped a uniformed representative who, after checking your credentials, would have rummaged valiantly under the bonnet of your example of British Leyland's finest workmanship. He might have to break the bad news that you might not see your bed for many hours - at least not by driving to it in the stricken Austin. The Allegro would have to be taken to a garage for repairs.

At least you wouldn't have to travel for miles in the car's brown vinyl driver's seat. The Bedford had a nice crew cab for you and any unfortunate passengers to travel in. Down would come the ramps and up on to the back of the beavertailed wrecker would go the Allegro. The Bedford would then travel along at a surprising lick, causing you occasionally to glance nervously behind to see if the Allegro was still there. And discover to your dismay that it still was.

If you were lucky, you'd be taken straight home and the car would be placed next to a line-up of Princesses and Minis at your friendly local BL dealer. If not, the car and yourself would be ferried to a "relay centre" where, with only other breakdown victims and a hot drinks machine for company, you'd have to wait for another AA truck which was travelling more in the direction you wanted to go.

AA INSP

Ready for work as well as winning shows.

Back lights are original. Essex registration number came from a car.

ECTION!

At least the AA man would leave you with a respectful salute. Or had they stopped saluting by then? They weren't still riding around on motorcycles and sidecars. Still, I hope all this sets the scene ...

The Bedford, said to have been one of the first four J-types of its, er type, bought by the AA, would have been a lynchpin of such situations for some 12 years before it ended up with a London dealer.

It was bought for £600 by Trevor Revell, who had worked on Bedfords since 1963, when he started with the construction company, William Press and Son Ltd in Tottenham. Today, Trevor and his son Woody are more involved with the marque than ever - and not just through having restored the beavertailed Bedford.

They've recently sold a commercial vehicle repair garage, TR Autos, Takeley,

Upgraded 330 turbo engine fitted.

J-type owner Woody Revell.

Restored and upgraded - 1974 former AA Bedford J-type.

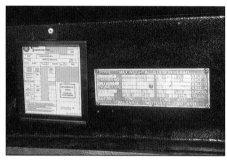

Replated.

Centre ramp to cope with three-wheelers!

Essex, near Stansted Airport, and set up the Bedford Motor Company Ltd.

"We've always loved Bedfords and enjoyed working on them so we thought we'd set up this new business. All manner of renovations, repairs and spares supply are now being carried out."

Yes, but what about this wrecker you ask? Well, the 1972 Bedford, originally VLG 959M, had been worked hard for more than 15 years, being used for the then family hobby of banger racing as well as in connection with the business.

One day, Woody came to a sudden conclusion: "I just looked at it and decided there were too many holes in it - too much ventilation," he recalled. The Bedford would not just be restored ... but transformed.

First task was to strip the lorry down to the chassis, which was found to have remained in excellent condition and only needed painting.

As restoration progressed, Woody and Trevor were offered a replacement cab which had been imported from Australia.

It gets better. The Bedford now has a turbocharged 130hp 330 Bedford engine instead of the original 300, this being mated to a five-speed automatic gearbox.

"It's very happy at 50mph but it'll pull itself up to 70 or more," Woody revealed.

Braking was also much improved with a conversion from vacuum to air hydraulic brakes, the "new" system coming from a Bedford TK.

The lorry has also been uprated to 7.5 tons, though the AA contributed to this by beefing up the springs. The rear axle has been uprated with a higher ratio differential, also adding to the J-type's impressive cruising capabilities.

The Bedford's capabilities have been further improved with a Desert Dynamics winch, made in America. The beavertail body is virtually original, though the lockers have been replaced with some from a Russian-built ZIL! Uprated "air-suspended" seats have also been fitted.

The lorry has been inspected by VOSA and recertified and is ready for a new career complete with

distinctive private registration number which has come from a car.

Er, haven't we missed something? Ah yes, the painting. After Trevor and Woody decided to get the Bedford ready for the 2005 Bedford Gathering, it was sent for a respray to Samurai Performance at Braintree, Essex. Now, bear in mind that the event was taking place on the following Sunday.

Over to Trevor: "On the Monday they painted it. Thursday night some of the windows went in, Friday the final three windows went in. They were a bit worried when I was putting the windscreen in. Being a toughened windscreen I was kicking it."

We wouldn't recommend you try that at home, or anywhere else, but we will bow to Trevor's considerable Bedford

Original beavertail body can cope with Porsches, Citroëns and other low-slung cars.

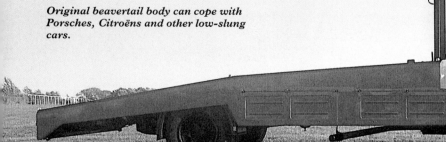

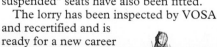

Bedford before its major restoration - note original registration number. (Photos courtesy the Revell family).

Lockers came from, of all things, a ZIL!

Replacement cab being reunited with renovated chassis.

experience!

Finally, the bumper was painted on the Saturday night before the show. The Bedford attended, starred and was voted best vehicle at the event. "I was well pleased," said Woody. Although much loved, the Bedford isn't just going to be a showpiece. "It will definitely get used," Woody adds.

The styling of the beavertail means the lorry will pick up low-slung vehicles such as Porsches and Citroëns without the considerable chocking normally needed, but it has a most useful feature which, to be honest had to be demonstrated before a cynical me. As you'll know, two ramps are slid into place to enable a car to be driven or winched on board, but the Bedford has three. "This meant that three-wheelers could be picked up easily," Woody explained.

So, if our unfortunate Allegro owner mentioned earlier had spent so much on car repairs that he decided to buy a

Reliant Robin, is still running around in it and breaks down in Essex, they might just be reunited with a certain Bedford J-type!

* The Bedford Motor Company Limited is on 07979 622548.

Engine bay gets its first coat of paint after priming.

Highly useful Desert winch.

Interior modifications included modern air-suspension seats.

"New" cab from Australia had survived well.

ENTOMBE

When Nick Larkin was invited to help retrieve a Morris lorry locked away for 40 years, he had no idea he'd find a unique survivor.

Finding Tutankhamun's tomb was merely stumbling across a few pieces of costume jewellery compared to this.

What a tale. A Morris lorry that had lain undisturbed in a barn for almost 40 years, needed to be removed as the building had been sold. I was invited to help with its retrieval.

I have to say that there's nothing quite the same as this type of investigation. What condition would the vehicle be in, and what was it? Would it contain priceless artefacts, or a fascinating piece of everyday lorry driver's life from the early 1960s? Equally intriguing is how the vehicle came to be laid up for so long. It's too big to lose, really.

Roger Shippey, whose family own the lorry, explained. The Morris had been bought new by his father, Henry, who with his brother, Sam, farmed as Sam Shippey and Sons. Henry, now 91, was the second generation in the business, which had been formed by his father, another Sam, in the early 1900s.

The firm is still in the family, Roger now running Newton Fruit farms based at Newton, near Wisbech, Cambs. He could well have supplied the apples you've just bought from a certain large supermarket.

Back to the lorry. "It was used largely for carting sugar beet in the winter from here to the Peterborough sugar factory, and in the summer carting peas to a pea viner. It was also used for carting corn and apples at harvest time and as a general runabout," recalls Roger.

"I remember before we had mains water laid on we would drive the Morris to Wisbech, loaded with open top tanks. There we'd get water from a stand pipe for the animals. With the tanks being open, we'd be lucky to get two-thirds of it back!"

Then mechanical disaster struck the Morris, though neither Roger or any of the family can recall exactly what.

"As I remember it went to a local garage. After it had been there for some weeks, things were getting critical on the farm as we needed a lorry. Spares were either unavailable or took a long time to come, and we ended up getting a new lorry, also a Morris.

"As far as we know, this one was towed to the shed using a tractor and left there awaiting spares. It's still waiting!"

So there we were outside the shed,

facing the formidable task of Morris extraction.

Roger did almost all the considerable work of shifting years of foliage (my feeble excuse: I was recovering from a bad cold and only one spade had been provided!).

Finally, the shed doors were gently prised open a few inches, carefully checking that the hinges would take the strain… then a little more, and a shadowy hulk could be seen inside.

Out came the sun and the Cambridgeshire registration number DJE 893 was highlighted. This led to renewed vigour in attacking the foliage until we could get inside. Greenery which would pass as jungle vines and creepers greeted us along with our prize – the Morris. Shame about the missing front grille panel. Oh there it is, propped near the front tyre… the still inflated tyre!

All these tales of the need to keep vehicles in an airy environment are true. Apart from bits of surface rust, the Morris was more intact than we'd dared assume – even in our most optimistic dreams. Had the engine been in situ, we'd probably have been able to drive the vehicle away.

More hacking away against the forces of nature revealed yet more Morris – no nasties on the chassis – and a wooden flat body in astonishingly sound condition. And as we climbed aboard, there was not a single splintering sound.

Rummaging through the undergrowth revealed a box of bits, including a dynamo and distributor, while over there was the radiator and

Unveiled after 40 years – the sole known Morris FVS.

Cab is far from rotten, with signwriting still intact.

Front grille panel located near the still inflated (!) tyre.

D MORRIS

THE UNEARTHING....

Dig for Morris. Roger Shippey attacking years of undergrowth around the building where Morris had reposed for 39 years.

Doors eventually give way revealing the registration number, but would the hinges stand up?

Getting better with one door open. Hope the ivy isn't poisonous!

Cab complete apart from instruments.

Revealed! Morris blinks in daylight for the first time since 1964.

Not a rally sticker but a souvenir from a visit to British Sugar at Peterborough in 1964.

Chassis looks extremely sound.

ah... the cylinder head, water jacket and a couple of pistons, complete with rods.

I couldn't help but compare this to the wreck of a ship, with wreckage spread over a wide area.

Then, in the very depths of the undergrowth, we found the block which looked remarkably intact. Definitely the basis of a rebuildable engine here – though, of course, a cracked head or block was a possibility.

I childishly decided to put the front grille back on before clambering excitedly into the cab, the door opening without problems.

Wow, thought I. No one's been in here for 40 years. Sadly the speedo was missing so I couldn't check the mileage. Look in the window, a paper sticker bearing the number 181 and the legend 'Peterborough 1964' was testament of the lorry's last trip to the British Sugar factory.

The driver's seat bears repairs made more than 40 years ago. Now was the time to rummage for everyday relics. Prize after prize came. A Senior Service cigarette packet (empty, and no Government health warnings), a receipt for storage crates returned, a Morris Commercial lubrication chart and a tin of Holt's 'Anti Squeak'.

It gets even better. Under the seat, bottles which once contained a Kia-Ora orange squash bottle and, equally empty, CWS Orange Drink. The driver must have liked his Vitamin C as a Lyons Maid Orange Kwench ice lolly wrapper also came to light.

Morris built the chassis, Willenhall the body.

'Ang on, what's this? A handbook for the FVS and FVSO range, and on the front bulkhead, two plates. One from Morris Commercial Cars Ltd., revealing the chassis number FVS 12/5R 9642 and the engine (or ex-engine) number being SEA 8659. The second, less legible plaque had been placed there by the Willenhall Motor Radiator Co Ltd., this presumably referring to the cab.

All this was almost too much to take in, but then we noticed a rather disturbing fact. It seemed that a main supporting beam of the barn was being supported... by

the sides of the lorry. An attempt to shift the Morris could have led to disaster. No moving out today, then!

Better get on the phone to find out more from the man who knows more about Morrises than just about anyone – the Morris Commercial Club's technical correspondent and archivist, Geoff Fishwick.

I explained the story only to be greeted by silence at the end of the phone, a silence of the sort you know isn't unfriendly, a silence which you expect to be punctuated by the sound of a china cup falling to the ground and smashing.

"That's an FVS," he said. "I'm really thrilled to bits. We don't know of any other survivors – in fact, we've been looking for one of these vehicles and appealed to members on several occasions to be on the lookout."

Geoff explained that the FVS was a six-cylinder version of the forward-control FV five-tonner introduced in 1948. From 1953, the FVS 12/5 (FV model, Six cylinder and 12ft 6in wheelbase/five tonner), and diesel version the FVSO 12/5 would succeed all other FVs.

From September 1953, the FV-style in-house coachbuilt cab with rear-hinged 'suicide' doors was superseded by the Willenhall-built cab (sometimes called Phase 2) with front opening doors, the front of the chassis being lowered to accept this.

The new cab was said to make it easier for drivers to reverse as they could open

The sheer 'everydayness' of 40 years ago – soft drink bottles, lolly wrapper, fag packet, lubrication chart, handbook, 'Anti Squeak' and receipt.

Early FV with coachbuilt cab, earlier style radiator and rear-hinged 'suicide' doors. The range began in 1948.

(Photo: Morris Commercial Club)

Undergrowth reveals the cylinder head and block.

Think radiator might just need some work.

the door to guide themselves. This cab would also be used on the Guy Invincible along with ERF and Dennis models. The Morris version also had the 'Pear Shape' front grille as seen on the early LD van.

DJE 893 would have been built in l954, the final FVS appearing in March 1955 when 10,058 of the FV family had been built. This final chassis number shows how few were FVS, but you'd think there would have been more than one survivor.

By the time you read this, the necessary barn supports will have been fitted and the Morris will be ready for a new owner, who

will hopefully restore it as sympathetically as possible.

The last word goes to Roger: "It's rather fun to see the Morris again, but it's such a waste having it sitting there. Someone ought to enjoy having it and working on it."

Serious enquiries on 01945 870254.

THANKS Many thanks to the Morris Commercial Club for all its help with this feature. The club can be contacted via Gordon Payley, 32 Daniell Way, Great Boughton, Cheshire CH3 5XH, tel: 01244 348908.

(Photo: Morris Commercial Club)

An early model FVS 12/5 of 1950, featuring coachbuilt cab and traditional radiator grille.

Body in excellent condition – note the discarded pistons.

(Photo: Morris Commercial Club)

New style cab and 'Pear Shape' grille came in 1953.

DOWN GO THE COSTS

With this NEW MORRIS FIVE-TONNER

LONG WHEELBASE — FORWARD CONTROL
WITH 16ft. 6in. INTERIOR BODY LENGTH

O.H.V. 6 CYLINDER PETROL ENGINE

How the brochure designers saw it!

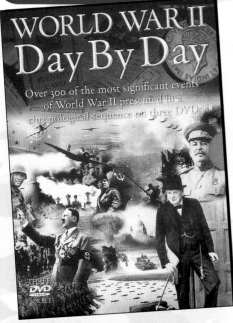
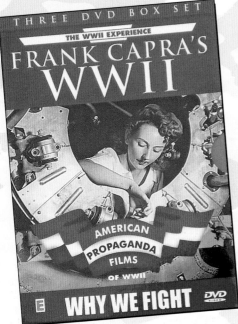

SUBSCRIBE

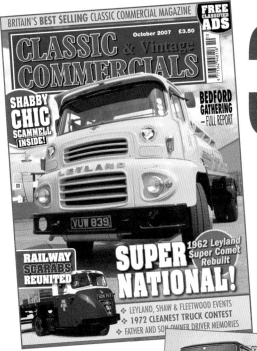

BRITAIN'S BEST SELLING CLASSIC COMMERCIAL MAGAZINE

FREE CLASSIFIED ADS

October 2007 £3.50

CLASSIC & Vintage COMMERCIALS

SHABBY CHIC SCAMMELL INSIDE!

BEDFORD GATHERING – FULL REPORT

RAILWAY SCARABS REUNITED

SUPER NATIONAL!

1962 Leyland Super Comet Rebuilt

❖ LEYLAND, SHAW & FLEETWOOD EVENTS
❖ 1972 CLEANEST TRUCK CONTEST
❖ FATHER AND SON OWNER DRIVER MEMORIES

THE POWER. AND THE GLORY.

Take the high road...

Prices correct at time of going to press

3 BIG REASONS TO SUBSCRIBE

1. Subscribe by direct debit and get CVC for only £3.20 an issue*
2. Delivered POST FREE direct to your door
3. Get a FREE A3 poster worth £6.99 with direct debit*

*UK only offer

FILL IN AND SEND THIS COMPLETED COUPON BACK TO:

(UK ONLY) CVC, Kelsey Publishing Group, FREEPOST SEA 2268, Westerham, Kent TN16 3BR.

(OVERSEAS) CVC, Kelsey Publishing Group, PO Box 13, Westerham, Kent TN16 3WT.

Telephone: 01959 541 444 or Fax: 01959 541 400
Email: cvc.info@kelsey.co.uk or Website: www.kelsey.co.uk

CLASSIC & Vintage COMMERCIALS — SUBSCRIPTION APPLICATION

Title: .... Initial:................ Surname:.................................

Address: ....

....

.... Postcode:.............................

E-mail: .... Telephone:.......................

Please send me poster No............. free with my direct debit subscription.

SAVE £1.80 BY DIRECT DEBIT

(UK SUBSCRIBERS ONLY) Normal price of 6 issues £21.00, you pay just £19.20 by DD every 6 months

---

KELSEY PUBLISHING GROUP

Instruction to your Bank or Building Society to pay by Direct Debit

 DIRECT Debit

Please fill in the form and send to: Kelsey Publishing, Freepost SEA 2268, Westerham, Kent TN16 3BR.

Name and full postal address of your Bank or Building Society

To: The Manager   Bank/Building Society
....

Address: ....

....

....

.... Postcode: ....

Name(s) of Account Holder(s): ....

Branch Sort Code

| ..... | ..... | ..... | ..... | ..... | ..... |

Bank/Building Society account number

| ..... | ..... | ..... | ..... | ..... | ..... | ..... | ..... |

Originator's Identification Number

| 8 | 3 | 7 | 3 | 8 | 3 |

Reference (official use only)

| C | V | C | ..... | ..... | ..... | ..... | ..... | ..... | ..... | ..... |

Instruction to your Bank or Building Society

Please pay Kelsey Publishing Ltd. Direct Debits from the account detailed in this instruction subject to the safeguards assured by the Direct Debit guarantee. I understand that this instruction may remain with Kelsey Publishing Ltd. and, if so, details will be passed electronically to my Bank/Building Society.

Signature: ....

Date: ....

Banks and Building Societies may not accept Direct Debit Instructions from some types of account.

SAVE £3.60 (12 ISSUES FOR THE PRICE OF 11)

12 month subscription: ☐ UK £38.40 ☐ Europe/Ireland £44.40 ☐ RoW £49.44

☐ **I WISH TO PAY BY CHEQUE**

I enclose my cheque for £.. (payable to Kelsey Publishing Ltd)

☐ **I WISH TO PAY BY CREDIT CARD**

Card Number: ....

Valid From: .... Expiry Date: .... Issue No. (Switch only): ....

Card holder: ....

Signature:.. Tel No.:..

If you DO NOT wish to receive information on related products or services, tick this box ☐   **CODE: CVC**

GRADE

I was during our photoshoot of last year's show-stopping 1947 Fordson Thames 7V that Paul Le-Strange introduced me to his 'other' project.

Tucked away in the corner of a shed and looking travel weary was an ERF A-series tractor unit. I was cheeky enough to ask Paul to let me know when he had finished work on it as I would like to photograph it as well. From the look of the lorry, I imagined it would be at least another two or three years, so I would have plenty of time to save up for another roll of film.

However, just after Christmas 2003, Paul called to say that work was progressing well and that he intended to complete the ERF in time for this year's London to Brighton Run. It wasn't too long afterwards that I found myself looking at another superbly restored lorry basking in the sunshine. The ERF looked magnificent and it was hard to believe that this was the same lorry I had seen only a few months earlier.

Mr WG Golding bought the 1975 A-series tractor from ERF agent WJ Boyes for £9600. It was used with tanker trailers transporting edible oil for Van den Bergh & Jurgens, and later operated on contract for a subsidiary of Unilever, carrying a Loders & Nucoline headboard on a regular run to Silvertown, Canning Town, in London.

In 1990, following many years of hard use, it was parked up and used as a static pump to transfer edible oil from the storage tanks into the tanker bodies ready for delivery. It eventually came back to Golding's yard in 1998 where it was finally laid up.

Paul Le-Strange's 1947 Fordson 7V was a major prizewinner at the London to Brighton Run and one of the most talked about lorries of the year. Now he's done it again with a highly contrasting vehicle, a 1975 ERF A-Series.

Report and photos: Alan Barnes.

A ERF!

All it needs is a trailer... coming soon.

Looking superb. Paul Le-Strange's 1975 ERF A-series tractor unit.

ERF in its service days, with tanker trailer.

A-post needed to be renewed.

Cab in fairly good overall condition.

Work on hubs underway.

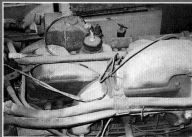

Cummins engine in generally good order.

This potted history misses out so much – not least the redoubtable character of the ERF's owner, his love for the lorry and the friendship forged between Paul and the Golding family.

Paul first encountered the ERF in his days as an apprentice with WJ Boyes. "Goldings, which had some 25 lorries at its peak, was a very big customer of Boyes," recalled Paul. "This ERF came in with a porous cylinder head and was losing water. I was 19 years old and Mr Golding was a fairly forceful sort of fellow. I was very worried about being given the job... I wasn't that enthusiastic about doing it.

"About five days after he collected the lorry, Mr Golding brought it back. He came up to me and said: 'Did you do my lorry?' I said 'Yes.' He said: 'Well, it's never ran better!' He gave me £25 as a drink – nigh on a week's wages then!

"From that day I've remained friends with the Golding family. Sadly, Mr Golding senior died recently, and they've just come out of the lorry business."

Paul pays tribute to Mr Golding, who is remembered with an inscription on the restored ERF. "He was what I call a proper wagon man – in haulage all his life.

"He had so many stories to tell: changing sprockets on chaindrive Scammells for example. He started working for a company in Barking as a trailer boy in a horse-drawn cart. He used to work for the Crow Carrying Co, and told how Mr Crow used to have a suitcase full of money and go up to Scammell in Watford to buy a new lorry."

Mr Golding was always a staunch traditionalist, even having, shall we say, a rather unique attitude towards putting indicators on lorries. "He thought indicators were a complete con, that they were only fitted to see more wiring and more bulbs. He said it didn't do bulbs any good, flashing on and off like that."

Mr Golding loved the ERF, keeping it after it was withdrawn from service and storing the lorry where he could see it from his window. "He made a big thing about that lorry. It was always his lorry," said Paul. "I offered to buy it off him and he said no. Before he passed away, he said anyone who helped the business should have something out of it, and so he left me the ERF."

Added Paul: "I think if the lorry had been restored when Mr Golding was still alive, he'd have ended up operating it."

When Paul went to collect the lorry, he found that it had suffered a little from being stored outside and was covered in green mould. He intended to just do a light restoration so that he could use the ERF with a low-loader, but it soon became obvious that more work would be required.

In 2002, he began the initial work. "The first thing I did was to get it running and driving, and generally tidy it up. I got some new rear lamp brackets made, the header tank was rusted off, so I replaced that." But then things changed for the worse. "It soon became obvious that a lot more work would be needed, and there was some serious rust."

At the time, Paul was busy completing the Fordson 7V. After this was finished in April 2003, Paul was able to concentrate on the ERF.

Most important to deal with was serious rusting to the underside of the cab and parts of the chassis. Most of the cab was in pretty sound condition, although the back timbers had to be replaced as did the wooden A-post on the driver's side. With that completed, the rest of the cab was tidied up and prepared for painting, and attention turned to the chassis.

Close inspection revealed some very bad corrosion under the fifth wheel. "The layers of rust built up and were pushing the chassis apart," said Paul. The chassis was stripped down to get at the affected areas, and some very hard work resulted in the removal of two buckets of rust!

"The whole chassis was cleaned and shot-blasted to remove every speck of rust and dirt in preparation for priming and painting."

Brakes were overhauled and re-lined and one of the front drums replaced. Shackle pins were replaced where required and the hub seals renewed. The gearbox was

ERF awaits currently under-restoration trailer!

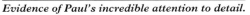

Evidence of Paul's incredible attention to detail.

Above: Chassis under fifth wheel was a major rot spot – not that you could tell now.

ERF reveals its builder's plate.

Chassis harboured some nasty corrosion, especially under fifth wheel.

Chassis and engine finished and awaiting cab.

Repairs to area under fifth wheel completed.

Paul with a definite classic commercial enthusiast of the future – his son, Jack, 4.

perfectly sound, as was the clutch – which Paul knew would be alright as he had fitted a replacement only 5000 miles before the ERF was taken off the road.

The original 220 Cummins engine was in good condition, despite some rumoured hard driving by Mr Golding senior when new. "It was in much better condition than I thought," said Paul.

Despite this, new big ends, liners and piston rings were fitted. Paul was also surprised to find that the sump had never been removed from the engine in its working years. The gearbox was also in good condition. It's a six-speed David Brown unit, a surprisingly traditional choice when most of these ERFs would have had Fuller range change units.

Explained Paul: "Mr Golding didn't like range change gearboxes as he felt there was a lot of piping to go wrong, and people didn't drive them properly. ERF had apparently said they didn't fit the David Brown 'box anymore, but Mr Golding said that if they couldn't supply one, he'd go for a Foden or Atkinson."

The interior was smartened up, but cleaning the seats required a good deal of elbow grease to get rid of spots of white emulsion that had dripped on them when the inside of the roof was painted some years previously. A friend of Paul's, Kelvin Healey, drew the short straw and spent nearly three months picking the tiny spots of paint out of the dimples in the upholstery.

A couple of fibreglass panels on the rear of the cab came from Rush Green Motors. Unfortunately, the original internal door pockets were beyond repair and as these items are almost impossible to find, two new pockets were made up by Ian Brown, another friend of Paul's. These were fitted to the doors at the second attempt as Paul dropped and broke them during his first effort at fixing them and they had to go back to Ian for repair.

Painting in Epsom green and red was carried out by Cruseley Trailers of Purfleet using two-pack on both the cab and chassis, while the neat and understated lining was completed by Astra Sign & Graphic Ltd. The ERF had been several colours in its career, including dark blue cab with red chassis, and latterly French blue. "I wanted to keep it in this blue, but Bill Golding said they had never liked it," recalled Paul.

Finding some of the spare parts for the A-series proved to be a problem. In fact, I was surprised when Paul told me that he found it a lot easier to get spares for the old Fordson than this 'modern' lorry. However, he managed to overcome this difficulty and the result is another superb piece of restoration. It will arguably be one of the best lorries to return to the road this year.

Paul intends to pair the tractor unit with a bulk tanker, which will become available later, and I am certain that the combination will create an impact on the rally scene.

In the morning we were joined by William Golding's son, Bill, who brought along his 1984 ERF E-series, D411 MVS, with a 1972 trailer which the firm had also bought new. The opportunity was taken to picture both vehicles side by side by way of comparison. Also joining us were Paul's wife, Sarah Jane, and their four-year-old son Jack. Despite

ERF with equally immaculate E-series owned by Bill Golding, son of the A-series' mentor William, and used to transport vintage tractors.

being on his way to playschool, he had insisted on wearing his smart new overalls and proudly told me that he would be riding with his dad in the ERF on the London to Brighton Run – a definite classic commercial enthusiast of the future there!

Talking of the future, Paul reckons that spares for 1970s' ERFs will become increasingly difficult to get. "During the restoration, I thought I'd be able to get parts from the people I'd always dealt with, but the stuff had gone. When people get into restoring lorries of this era, they're going to struggle. In some ways, the Fordson was easier to restore – most stuff could be made, but when you start getting into these 1970s' vehicles, there's lots of fibreglass and plastics."

Not surprisingly, the ERF took an award at Brighton, finishing third in the tractor unit section. Paul's Fordson also did well, coming first the Ford category. A 1969 trailer owned by the Golding family, which ran for WG Golding and would have been towed by the A-series in its service days, is currently under restoration and will be rallied alongside the ERF.

Concludes Paul: "You'll never find another ERF like this – it was so original and it brings back so many lovely memories of a great character and lorry man."

So, will Paul be restoring a third vehicle? "Well, I've said no at the moment, but there is an Atkinson Borderer with a Gardner 180 engine…" Watch this space!

THANKS

Thanks are due to Paul for his help with this feature, Bill Golding for covering the early history, and to Tim Benton for allowing us to take the pictures around the farm.

PS… The big question – will Paul be restoring a third vehicle. "Well, I've said no at the moment, but then there is an Atkinson Borderer with a Gardner 180 engine. Watch this space!

Paul's superb 1947 Fordson Thames 7V did well at London-Brighton.

Lorry finished in green, matching Thames 7V.

*This 1979 Leyland
Buffalo has been restored
to represent a decade of a
family firm's history.
Alan Barnes reports.*

(Photos: Alan Barnes)

I t wasn't the happiest start for
a newly restored vehicle.
Andrew Davies' beautifully
presented 1979 Leyland
Buffalo was due to make its debut
on the 200 Great West Road Run.
"It seemed to be running as sweet
as a nut, but 10 miles after leaving
home, the engine seized," Andrew
recalls. "TL11 engines are prone to
carbon build-up and the lorry had
been standing around for a long
time."

So the engine was meticulously rebuilt
over the winter. Andrew reckons all the
extra effort was worthwhile when the lorry
finally made its sparkling debut at this
year's CTP A-Z Road Run.

JFD 48V was supplied new by Brownhills
Commercials to Staffordshire Farmers Ltd
of Wolverhampton, and was allocated to the
firm's depot at Allscott, Telford.
Staffordshire Farmers ran a fleet of over 80
vehicles which included five Leyland
Buffalo which operated out of their depots
throughout the Midlands. They were
primarily used for agricultural transport
which included grain, feeds, fertiliser and
livestock. During its life with Staffordshire
Farmers, JFD 48V was driven by John
Eccleston and used to collect grain from
farms and delivering the loads to Allscott
Depot's seed cleaning department.

In August 1984, the Buffalo, along with
numerous Leyland Clydesdales, Bisons,
flats and bulk blowers, was bought by
Albert Davies (Transport) Ltd, a company
started in 1928 by the uncle of the present
managing director and owner of the

*Leyland is part of a family history
stretching back to 1928.*

*Looking superb down to the finest
detail is 1980 Leyland Buffalo.*

FFALO
TORED

Leyland not so happy after years standing in the yard.

Buffalo in shunting days.

Too far gone – original cab removed from chassis.

Starting with the chassis. Strangely, the electrics survived well.

Much work needed at this stage!

No, this isn't the respray, but further evidence of the amount of preparation going into this lorry.

Buffalo, Albert Davies. Albert died in 1942 and Fred, Andrew's father, took over. Fred is still active in the firm today.

Vehicle wise, the firm started with a four-cylinder Chevrolet, moving onto a six-cylinder example. Bedfords were followed by Commer Q4s, a move being made to Leyland Comets after the war.

Leylands and Albions were the backbone of the fleet until the late 1970s, when Mercedes began to gain favour. Nowadays a variety of makes is operated, though there has been a shift towards Volvo. The company is still at its original Acton Burnell depot, near Shrewsbury. Various aspects of agricultural haulage were carried out over the years, but the company now specialises in bulk animal feeds.

Coaches were operated for many years until 1965 and FAW 334, a Plaxton-bodied Crossley, bought new in 1948, has been retained.

All the lorries, with the exception of the Buffalo and a Leyland Bison Bulk blower LDH 970V, were refurbished in their workshops and sold on. The Buffalo was employed as a shunter by their sister company, Bulkrite, and used to ferry trailers to and from the sandblasters at Ellesmere and to collect customer's trailers for body repairs.

A few weeks' use confirmed that the Leyland was in excellent

mechanical order but that the cab had all the usual problems of rot under the windscreen, on the doors and wings and around the rear corners. With a bit of work, the unit could be promoted from its mundane yard duties.

The chassis was sandblasted and painted and a replacement cab from one of the fleet's old Leyland Octopus was fitted and repainted. It was then taxed and used by the company as an experiment to see if artics would be more versatile in the feed delivery fleet. Until that time, only six-and eight-wheel bulkers had been used. The unit was used to transport sugar beet to the British Sugar factory at Allscott and also for transporting bulk feeds all over the Midlands. The experiment was considered a success, and the company added to its artic fleet by buying in Mercedes 1625, 1628 and 1635. The Leyland remained in active use until 1986/87, when it once more reverted to use as a yard shunter.

Andrew recalls: "Over the years, it got the abuse that all shunters get, and eventually one windy day when it was being driven out of the workshop, a gust of wind blew the roof clean off, and most of the interior plastic trim disappeared as well."

The roof was recovered and fixed back on with fibreglass and the Leyland soldiered on in the yard until it was eventually replaced by a 1986 Leyland Roadtrain 6x2.

The battered old Buffalo was finally laid up in 1997. Parked in a corner of the workshop, it

Ergomatic cab is an updated version of the unit dating back to the mid-1960s.

Now this is what we call attention to detail.

In the sprayshop, where two-pack paint was applied.

Rear of cab needed a lot of preparation to get to this stage.

Replacement cab ready for outer panels to be replaced.

Chassis after sandblasting and painting.

Cab was restored using various pieces of trim saved over the years.

was forgotten about until 2002 when Andrew decided to carry out a restoration. The cab was removed and the engine and gearbox taken into the workshop. As he observed, "the chassis was in pretty good condition probably due to the amount of oil it was covered in". After steam cleaning, the mechanical work was carried out with workshop mechanic Tony Allen, fitting new brake linings, hub seals, diaphragm and bearings.

The cab was too far gone for any sort of repair to be attempted, so a replacement was bought. Remembers Andrew: "I'd searched all over the country for a cab, and it suddenly struck me that Dorrington Sand, based about 100 yards from our depot, might have one. They did!"

Although not in mint condition, it was pretty sound. Having said that, the wings had to be rebuilt around the step area and the intermediate panels between the wings and the cab had to be made from scratch. Andrew fitted new wheelarches, replaced the guttering around the roof and replaced a few panels, doing most of the welding himself. The windscreen surround was in excellent condition and needed no repairs. With the help of Fred Palmer, another company employee, the minor cracks were filled and the cab was made ready for painting.

The company livery of olive and Cactus Green has been used since 1965, and Andrew painted the cab himself. The chassis was prepared by Fred, and Andrew gave it four coats of primer and five coats of colour using ICI two-pack. Tony Allen and Bob Mathews re-fitted the engine to the chassis and after the fifth wheel, diesel tank, air tanks and wheels were fitted, it was given one final coat of paint.

Andrew's son Robert helped re-fit the interior, and the work included replacing all of the internal plastic trim which had been lost or damaged over the years. As Andrew said: "Luckily we managed to make up a complete set of trim from various cabs that we had collected over the years. We'd scrapped better cabs than this."

With the rebuild largely completed and the basic paintwork finished, the signwriting was completed by Roy Bickley of Market Drayton, who has been painting the company's vehicles since the late 1960s.

The fifth wheel was thoroughly overhauled. Surprisingly, the Buffalo's wiring was in excellent condition. With the restoration completed, the Leyland was taken for its MoT and passed with flying colours.

For the A-Z Run, the Buffalo was paired with a 1973 M&G trailer, which again had been bought by Staffordshire Farmers as a tipping trailer for grain. They had it fitted with blowing equipment by Murfitt of Wisbech around 1978, and it was used until being sold to Albert Davies Ltd in 1987. It was then used for poultry food deliveries, teamed with a Mercedes 1628 tractor unit.

When the company used tri-axle trailers, the old one was sold. "Ironically, the farmer that bought it from us came back a few years later and needed a tri-axle blower! So I duly

TECHNICAL DETAILS
Leyland Buffalo 2

Chassis No:	7901175
Model Number:	4BU 11A 32
Engine:	TL11A
Engine Number:	TL11A/4/27960528
Gearbox:	Fuller RTO609A
First Registration:	August 13, 1979

Out on the road: TL11 engine gives Leyland a fair turn of speed.

Buffalo seen with appropriate 1973 trailer.

Master signwriter Roy Bickley applies his craft.

At last, the finished tractor unit.

sold him one of our early stepframe tri-axle blowers and took the M&G tandem back in part-exchange." The trailer was only used occasionally for smaller jobs and then rented out on spot hire until it was parked up while the work on the Buffalo was completed.

No major work has been done on the trailer apart from painting the body and the chassis, and even the blowing equipment is in good working order and could be used if required.

Andrew and his team can be well pleased with their restoration as the Buffalo and its trailer make a superb combination and are already scheduled to attend a number of events, having made a great impression at the Classic Commercial Motor Show at Gaydon.

As for future projects, well, Andrew is pressing on with building a preserved fleet. An Albion Reiver bought new by his firm, TAW 677J, was restored for the Albion Centenary and has been seen at several events since. He's also working on what is believed to be the last Leyland Octopus to be registered, which was bought by Davies in 1980 but not put on the road until 1986, as D567 PUX. It was later fitted with a Leyland Cruiser cab, operating until around 1994 and sold as a chassis cab to a buyer in Hereford.

"Since I sold it, the Octopus has not been used, so I intend to re-fit the Ergomatic cab and I still have its original bulk blowing body, which I shall re-furbish and fit," he said.

Andrew has several other projects, not least a Seddon 32/4 awaiting attention, and a recently withdrawn Volvo F10. "What I would like to do is to have one vehicle from each decade the company's been in business." Now that is going to be some fleet!

WANTED Andrew is looking for a LAD-cabbed Albion Reiver. Anyone who can help is invited to call him on 01743 718232.

VEHICLE

Bought for preservation for £1 in 1965, this 1935 Leyland Hippo has finally been restored. Nick Larkin reports

Photos: Nick Larkin

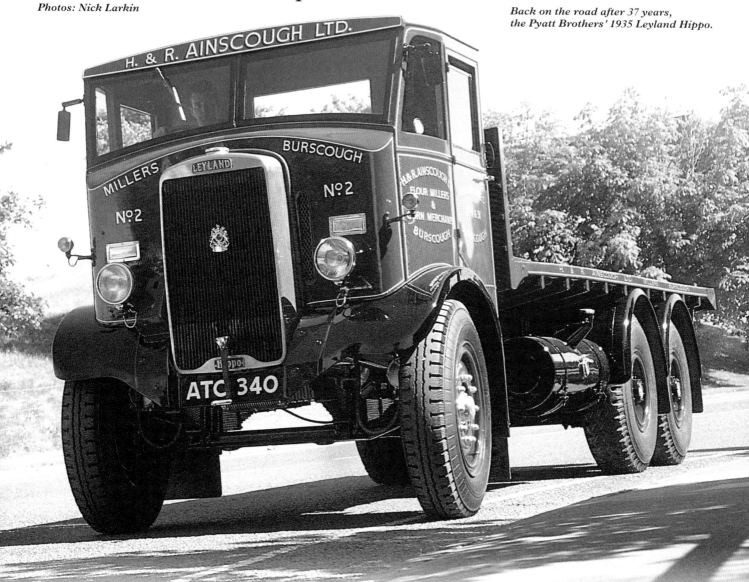

Back on the road after 37 years, the Pyatt Brothers' 1935 Leyland Hippo.

"**W**ould a pound be all right?" Those words, from the owner of a Lancashire flour mill, resulted in a 1935 Leyland Hippo being bought for preservation 40 years ago. In 1968, ATC 340 was taken off the road and now - finally - it's been restored to become a star of the 2005 rally season.

The Hippo has certainly had a chequered career, 30 years of it spent operating for the original owner, H and R Ainscough Ltd, of Burscough, Lancs. As a bouncing two-year-old, ATC's career was almost terminated after it hit a railway bridge after descending Parbold Hill, near

Burscough, a little quicker than was intended. The Hippo was returned to Leyland where it was fitted with a new cab, and a lot of work was carried out on the chassis. The original petrol engine was replaced with an 8.6 litre diesel unit.

In yet another testimony to the quality of mid-1930s Leylands, the Hippo remained in service until 1965, when it spent the summer on loan to a motor museum at Trentham Gardens, Stoke-on-Trent.

It was seen there by the late Gordon Pyatt, who made inquiries and was invited to discuss the matter at th'mill.

Neil Steele, who accompanied Gordon on the trip said: "I remember we were ushered into the mill owner's palatial office. He was quite a tall, thin man with dark hair. He asked for the ledger and

wondered what the lorry could be put down for."

One pound later the lorry was Gordon's. "It had been standing, but we put a new battery on and five gallons of fuel in and Gordon drove it home."

The Leyland turned out to be in useable condition, and quite presentable after a good polish. A set of original spec headlights were found, and the Hippo was taken to several rallies.

"Even in the mid-60s it attracted a lot of attention," recalled Neil, who today is particularly well known for his fire engine restorations, but in 1965 owned a Leyland Lion. Gordon Pyatt was already a seasoned restorer with, among other things, a Morris Commercial bought in 1958, a recovery vehicle new to John

POUND

Signwriting as original. The mill building still stands.

Brothers Simon, Robert and Mark Pyatt.

Pepper of Hanley, Stoke-on-Trent.

In 1968, the Hippo was taken off the road. "There wasn't a particular reason for this. I think it was really just that there were so many other vehicles around, said Neil, a lifelong Leyland fan and marque expert. He remains a friend of the Pyatt family and would act as advisor during the Hippo's restoration by Gordon's sons Anthony, Simon, Mark and Robert - renowned as the Pyatt Brothers with something like 15 restored Leylands between them.

Mark Pyatt continues the story: "We threatened to restore the Hippo for years but got involved with so many different things. It always started when we needed to move it but apart from that, it just stood in a shed."

He admitted: "It was the state of the cab that put us off. We can do metalwork and things like that but all the woodwork the Hippo needed meant that other projects tended to take precedence. All the joints had gone on the cab and they'd just been patched up."

About six years ago, a start was finally made for, say the brothers, several reasons. "We felt the time had come, I think. Maybe we felt that if we didn't restore the lorry now we never would. At least it was complete, but just sort of worn out."

Drastic action was called on for the cab. It was sent to have the framework rebuilt by Mick Sharpe, in Derby, renowned for his work on Rolls-Royces.

Most of the chassis turned out to be in good condition after shotblasting. An exception was the aluminium subframe which sits inside the chassis, with the back suspension bolted through it. The subframe was remade in steel, both for ease and cost reasons.

Side raves of original body needed much straightening!

The suspension was stripped down and rebuilt, the springs being overhauled. The brakes were also rebuilt. A split on the engine block was repaired and the unit overhauled. Mark rewired the lorry, which he said was fairly straightforward.

The original wooden body was rebuilt. A new floor, along with back and front crossmembers, were fitted, although the runners and bearers were good enough to be replaced. After much work, the side raves were straightened.

Once reframed, the cab was repanelled and the original interior woodwork shotblasted to remove the old varnish and then revarnished and polished by Anthony. New instruments were fitted as necessary and the seats reupholstered.

Painting was carried out in two-pack, beginning with etch priming and then - in a very thorough job - three or four undercoats and four topcoats! New glass was fitted and the cab signwritten by Steve Wooding. A nice touch was replacing the Leyland 'By Appointment' badge on the radiator.

Tyres, 42x9s, were a major problem: "It took us five years to find them - then we found two sets within two weeks, through adverts and finding out people who had them," Mark recalled.

A major task was making up a roadworthy wheel for the lorry, by riveting part of another wheel on to the original and drilling it out.

A new rear diff, found in an ex-military vehicle, was fitted, giving the lorry a top speed of some 35mph as opposed to the previous 20. Even in the 1960s, wear had been noticed in the rear axle.

Finally, the Hippo was ready for the road, making its rally debut at the 2005 Classic Commercial Motor Show - its first

Original cab reframed.

TIPS FOR RESTORERS

The Pyatt Brothers suggest:

1 **Don't start something unless you feel you can finish it.**

2 **Make sure that when you take something off a vehicle you put it where you know you can find it! Store things together, otherwise you can spend weeks trying to find something.**

3 **Get to know other enthusiasts.**
So many things are found by word of mouth!

4 **Never assume there are loads of spares around. Don't forget it is getting hard to find things for earlier vehicles now.**

Hippo when new with H and R Ainscough, flour millers and corn merchants, Burscough, Lancs.

Wonderful radiator badge showing that Leylands were 'By Appointment.'

event for 37 years. It's hoped at some point soon to take the Hippo back to Burscough, where the original H and R Ainscough mill still stands.

As Mark said, the lorry is very much part of the Pyatt family history. "When my brother Simon was two he was left in the cab and knocked the handbrake off. The Hippo rolled back and thankfully the kerb stopped it - otherwise it would have hit the local pub!"

Speaking for all the brothers, Mark said: "The Hippo was always there when we growing up, Dad saved it, and it was always one of his favourite lorries. We wanted to see it restored for his sake. We certainly all thought of him when we were doing the work."

Above & above right: On display at Trentham Gardens, Stoke-on-Trent, shortly before being bought for £1.

Chassis stripped and suspension rebuilt.

Removed from shed for restoration, 1999.

Engine block was repaired.

Head-on view is definitely imposing!

Cab before removal from chassis.

Cab in primer ready for refitting.

RESTORA MASTERS

In the second part of our 90th anniversary tribute to Bristol Commercial Vehicles, we look at the restoration of a second British Road Services lorry, this time a 1955 HG6L eight-wheeler. Many felt the vehicle had been past saving, but restorer Robin Masters, who waited 10 years to buy it, knew better...

Bristol used several makes of cab, but this is a BBW example built in-house.

Many dissenters said this 1955 Bristol HG6L was too far gone to restore. They've been proved wrong.

Robin Masters comes over as a modest man. He must, though, feel proud of his achievement in bringing a derelict 1955 Bristol HG6L eight-wheeler back to life. "I have always had a fascination for BRS wagons," he explains. "Especially eight-wheelers. I had not planned to actually own one, but the opportunity came up and I felt I had to take it."

We can all be thankful that Robin made that decision and can now enjoy seeing a rare example of the early type of HG6L with BBW cab and body. His efforts were rewarded at this year's Classic Commercial Motor Show where the Bristol won the award for the Best British Road Services Vehicle.

Robin and his fellow lorry enthusiasts used to go to rallies in the early Eighties as well as visiting haulage yards in search of interesting lorries. He recalls: "One day in 1983, we had been to Moreton C Cullimore's yard and were on our way home when we decided to visit Watson's scrap yard at Wadborough.

"I had been told they had a Bristol eight-wheeler in a rough state. My friends looked at it and said: 'That's no good – it's too far gone.'"

The proprietor of the yard was a bit reclusive and lived on site in a railway container. When Robin asked if he was interested in selling the Bristol, he was given the blunt reply: "No, I ain't!"

Although the Bristol looked pretty rough, it was fairly complete and Robin thought more and more about the possibility of restoring it. Every couple of years or so he would look in on Watson's to see if it was still there. This dragged on for 10 years and, of course, the poor old Bristol was at the mercy of the elements all that time.

In 1993, Robin was working as a driver

(Report and Pictures: Peter Davies)

TION
LASS

Robin Masters with the result of a superb restoration job.

EK9

BRITISH ROAD SERVICES

ROG 687

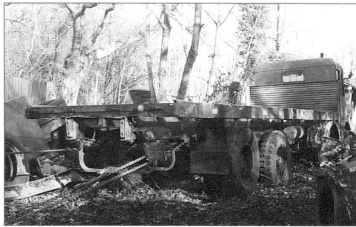

A wet November Friday and the Bristol, complete with stuck-on rear brakes, is about to be winched from its resting place of some 25 years.

It took much shuffling and most of the day to get the lorry to the stage where it could finally be winched onto the low loader.

Hiding much of its restoration horrors, the Bristol arrives at its new home. It was bucketing down with rain, of course!

Ready for repaint with new doorskins, body raves and replacement fibreglass panels.

Doors had to be reskinned as part of the restoration.

Dummy load of about two tons correctly sheeted down is said to reduce bounciness in the lorry's riding standards.

at Vic Haines of Pershore. One day, a driver tipped him off that Watson's yard was being cleared and if he wanted the Bristol, he would have to be quick as the yard was nearly empty. He rushed over to find the lorry he wanted so much was the only thing left.

It transpired that Mr Watson gone to live with his sister, letting the yard to a new occupant. "You'd better make your mind up quick," he told Robin, " 'cos it'll be cut up tomorrow!" Having waited so long, Robin wasn't going to lose the Bristol now so he offered the man £1000, which was readily accepted.

Next Robin spoke to his good friend and fellow restorer Garry Hill, Vic Haines' transport manager, and he agreed to help bring the Bristol back to the sanctuary of a farm building rented by Robin and three other enthusiasts.

In true British tradition, the weather was cold, dull and wet on the day of the move. Well, it was November!

"We went in Garry's Atkinson to fetch the Bristol one Friday, using Vic Haines' low loader", recalls Robin. "Neither Garry nor myself were at our best. We had been to the Transport Manager of the Year awards the previous day at the RAC Club at Pall Mall in London. We got back home in the early hours of Friday, so we'd had hardly any rest."

The first job was to winch the derelict truck from its resting place where it had lain for about 25 years. Using Turfer winches, the

Replacement glassfibre front panels came with the lorry and were duly fitted.

Don't even ask if there's a heater!

lads gradually dragged the rusting hulk into a more accessible position. Garry's Atkinson unit then hauled it out on to the road.

The rear brakes were seized on, which made life even more difficult. Once the Bristol was on the road, the Atkinson was again used to drag it up on to the low loader for the journey home.

"What with the rotten weather and the difficult access, it took us nearly all day," says Robin. "It was dark by the time we got back to Offerton to unload it."

On Saturday the weather was just as bad – it was throwing it down with rain, but ROG was duly pushed into the relative calm of the building. Garry uttered the immortal words, "I wonder if it'll go?" Diesel engines are surprisingly good at surviving years of neglect. Doubtless the oily properties of diesel fuel and the airtight fuel system help. It's amazing how long a diesel can stand and still fire up. ROG 687's Leyland O.600 was about to be put to the test.

The lads rigged a gallon can of fuel to feed into the pump and hooked a pair of big 12-volt batteries up. Robin tried filling the radiator, but that was full of leaks. However, there was oil in the sump.

To everyone's amazement, the engine fired up almost at once in a cloud of smoke. At least they now knew that it was a runner.

Surprisingly, the Bristol was so good mechanically that very little work was needed on the engine and gearbox. All the same Robin, with the support of various fellow enthusiasts, spent six years on the restoration. "I wanted to get it right," he explains. "I wanted it to go back exactly as it was with BRS."

In his quest for accuracy, Robin found out what he could about its history. It appears she was new to Birmingham Cheapside in June 1955 as Fleet No. 4E832. She was later transferred to Kidderminster and spent most of her working life hauling steel between South Wales and Austin's factory at Longbridge.

There were six Bristol eight-wheelers engaged on this work – three loading steel out of Port Talbot and three returning from Longbridge with baled scrap from the press shops. A changeover was made at Penarth Road, Cardiff, as the journey was too long to complete within the daily driving hours limit.

Robin put an advertisement in the local Kidderminster paper to find out more and two ex-drivers, Les Collins and Fred Brooks, replied. Les's recollections came in particularly useful in explaining a mystery surrounding the differential. "When we drained the oil from the axle, there were bits of metal in it," recalls Robin. "We withdrew the diff and one lump of metal was obviously a tooth from

Mileometer mounted outside the vehicle so the mileage could be easily checked.

EK9

Body raves, or side rails, had been damaged past salvaging. Replacements were sourced with the help of another Bristol restorer, Dave Tarbuck.

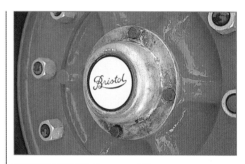

the crownwheel. The other two bits we couldn't identify.

Les explains what happened. He was heading to South Wales one night, fully laden with scrap, and a halfshaft went as he was going through Ledbury. He had to get the fitters out with a new halfshaft. The bits of metal Robin found were splines that had broken off and been knocked through when the new halfshaft was fitted. Evidently it was one of these broken off splines that had caused the tooth to break off the crownwheel.

The old Bristol served 11 years of hard graft but, along with most of its stable mates, it was withdrawn from service in 1966 and auctioned off.

ROG 687 was one of 517 Bristol HG6L rigid eight-wheelers built between 1952 and 1958. All were powered by Leyland O.600 six-cylinder diesel engines similar to that of the Leyland Octopus. Bristol fitted their own gearboxes and drive axles.

The first two sanctions, 88 and 96, featured a variety of cabs from ECW (Eastern Coach Works), Homalloy, Burlingham, BBW (Bristol's own Body Building Works) and MCW (Metro Cammell Weymann).

Robin's vehicle, 96010 (the 10th vehicle of the 96th sanction), had a BBW cab which was a composite structure based on an aluminium framework with aluminium panelling to the back and side panels. The front panelling, roof and wings were made in glassfibre, mainly to keep down tooling costs as well as saving weight. Another benefit of glassfibre is that it can be easily repaired.

A great deal of restoration work had to be done to both the cab and body. The doors had to be re-skinned and new glassfibre front panels, which came with the vehicle as purchased from Watson's, were duly fitted.

The body itself was particularly rough – four of the aluminium crossbearers were broken and the distinctive Bristol side raves had been damaged – not only by years of hard work, but by Watson fitting sides to the flat body.

Dave Tarbuck, a name that always crops up when Bristol is mentioned, came to the rescue with replacement raves. He had had some manufactured specially when restoring his own eight-wheeler, 221CWL. The raves are of a special section peculiar to Bristol, quite different from any of the standard sections available from aluminium stock holders.

The keroin decking was completely renewed – that alone cost £500. Robin is not one of the 'cheque book' restorers we hear about. He has to watch the pennies. He reckons the whole budget for the job was about £4000.

In a curious way, the end product has benefited from not being overdone. Bill Mills at Gloucester did the spray job in Ayres Red and black. The signwriting is cut-out vinyl lettering.

Robin has taken great care to restore the Bristol to its characteristic British Road Services' guise using the period door crests and what was its last known fleet number. The lorry is clean but not over restored. To

complete the effect, he keeps the vehicle loaded with a correctly roped and sheeted load which he varies from time to time to good effect.

"It also helps to take some of the bounce out of the ride," says Robin. "It is only a couple of tons, but it makes the ride a lot smoother."

He accepts that the new sheet looks a bit bright at the moment, but he points out that it will mellow in time and will look even more in keeping when it does further testimony of Robin's dedication to accuracy, which has served him so well.

Bristol is authentic right down to the sheeting used to secure the load, though owner Robin Masters feels this needs to weather a bit in the interests of authenticity.

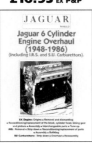

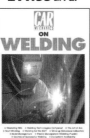

KIN

King Regent! If ever there v
1947 AEC Mammoth Majo
(Photos: Nick Larkin)

Remember chemistry lessons at school? Never my most successful subject - I'm certainly not off to probe some microbes in the lab when I've finished writing this.

The lessons could be fun though, even to the most stupid. After a few minutes of

*All you want from a vintage lorry?
Ward Jones's wonderful 1947 AEC
Mammoth Major II.*

T OIL COMPANY LTD

YF 16·

790

G REGENT!

*a lorry to sum up the appeal of classic commercials, it must be this truly joyous
w the subject of a model from EFE. Nick Larkin hears its fascinating story.*

unintelligible figures and squiggles scratched on the blackboard in chalk, and some equally mysterious long words being quoted, it was time for the "Practical Demonstration", ie, something interesting. Here was the chance to make a lot of noise, attack something with the naked flame of a Bunsen burner, change the colour of something and maybe even cause it to fizz.

The hoped for major explosion, or what a local paper might describe as a "human torch drama" never actually materialised, but your attention was still held. As a result, you even worked out what was supposed to be learned from the lesson.

These reminiscences came into my head the moment I set eyes on Ward Jones' wonderful 1947 AEC Mammoth Major. If

ever there was a vehicle which could give someone a "Practical Demonstration" of the appeal of classic commercials, or why on earth someone would want to buy, preserve and restore an old lorry, this vehicle must surely be it.

Imagine if Ward were to hire the vehicle out for "therapy" sessions. Dissenting lorry-hating spouses cured at a stroke. A couple

Eight-wheeler is perfectly propo[rtioned]

of years later, she'll be judging at the Classic Commercial Motor Show.

Owners of dull, modern 4x4s must happily wave this lorry on ahead of them rather than hit new levels of road rage being stuck behind it. So why this appeal?

Well the styling is nigh on perfect, from the curve of the wings, to the tapering of the cab, to the huge radiator, to the eight wheels.

It's also large, which will appeal to those who like particularly big toys, and it's an extremely rare example of a fuel tanker, with all those motoring connotations. It's also so British - the red, white and blue livery, with gold Regent lettering. And if that wasn't enough, there's even a Royal Warrant on the doors.

And what a wonderful registration number, KYF 16. And then the

wonderfully melodic AEC sound the lorry makes in action - it's not the loudest lorry around but my goodness does it make you listen! Don't just take my word for this. Exclusive First Editions (EFE), a leading producer of diecast models, has just added this very lorry to its range.

It's a strange experience, writing a story about a lorry while running a model of the very vehicle across your desk and attempting to replicate AEC engine noises and brake squeal. (Err... actually I meant closely inspecting the detail of this 1:76 scale replica).

As EFE's chairman, Frank Joyce, says about the decision to reproduce the lorry: "We came across this splendid preserved vehicle and thought it would be too good an opportunity to miss, knowing our collectors would love a model of this vehicle."

The AEC was anything like splendid when Ward bought it, however, but if anyone could restore this wreck, he could. Proprietor of Ward Jones Commercials, High Wycombe, Bucks, he's been working on large diesel engines for 45 years.

He left school in 1960 to start work as "a boy mechanic" with a corn and seed merchant, leaving 18 months later to join a family firm of fruit and vegetable merchants.

"They had an extremely diverse fleet, including Commer TS3 two-strokes, which took a bit of getting used to," Ward recalls. After a hard day's work getting to grips with such beasts, Ward studied at college in the evenings, gaining a certificate in mechanical engineering.

But suddenly, Armageddon struck. "After another mechanic left, I found myself in

Special permission was needed to show the Royal Warrant.

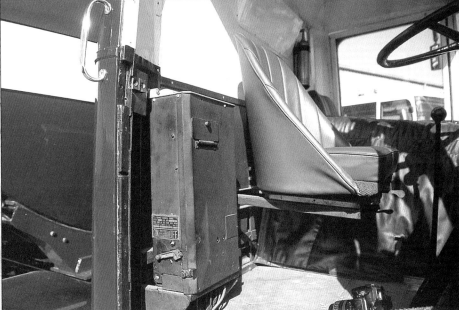

New control box found to replace burnt out original.

Attention to detail is astounding!

Catwalk replaced.

. Some wheels came from London trolleybuses!

charge of 36 vehicles. I had a struggle keeping them on the road, but also had to repair machinery, not least the carbide bird-scaring guns." But Ward persevered, and even gained a transport manager's licence.

Then in 1977, his employers bowed to pressure from supermarkets and closed, leaving Ward redundant. Later that year he took the plunge and set up the firm he still runs. Always a bus as well as a lorry enthusiast, he started buying and selling psvs as well as repairing commercials and selling parts. Business has continued to grow ever since, Ward Jones Commercials nowadays having a staff of eight.

Classic and working commercials remain a major part of the business and such is the diverse range of skills among the staff that almost anything can be carried out. Despite High Wycombe not exactly being typical

recruiting territory for a vehicle repair business, Ward has managed to recruit some younger staff.

"There is a shortage of people willing to get their hands dirty but everyone here is really enthusiastic. We are fortunate as we can turn our hands to anything - electrical, bodywork, wiring - the lot, and are happy to do so." All these skills and more certainly came in handy during the transformation of KYF 16.

One of seven examples delivered to the Regent Oil Company in 1947, the lorry originally worked from Canvey Island,

Essex. "We assume that it came out of service in 1967/8 as there is no evidence of it being plated after that," Ward told me. "Regulations at the time meant that with no brakes on the second axle it would have to have been downgraded if it was still to be used." The multi-pull ratchet handbrake was also well out of date by then.

Meanwhile, Regent Oils had been taken over by Texaco to form the basis of the American company's British operations. KYF 16 was taken to Pembroke Dock where it was fitted with a pump and a branch manifold and used as a fuel bowser

Cab defines its era.

RESTORATION IN PICTURES

Lorry had been through several owners ... but no work done!

AEC arrives for restoration behind Ward Jones's fine Atkinson wrecker.

Off with the cab.

Cab needed major surgery.

Down to the chassis, with cab and tank removed.

Virtually all cab framework renewed.

Much evidence of neglect inside cab.

Owners can't wait to get behind the wheel of a restored vehicle!

Chassis repaired and repainted.

Taking shape with rebuilt cab in place.

Original 9.6 litre AEC engine needed work and was replaced by 11.3 for spares and availability reasons.

Restoration supremo Ward Jones.

for ships. Later it fulfilled a similar role at Cardiff Docks before passing through several owners in preservation.

Ward, who also owns two beautifully restored buses, DBL 154, a 1946 former Thames Valley ECW-bodied Bristol K-type, and CFN 104, a 1947 Park Royal-bodied Leyland PS1, ex-East Kent, decided he really wanted a lorry.

"I wanted an eight-wheel lorry but not really a tanker as I knew there would be so much work to do on one. But this lorry was for sale locally, and tankers like this are rare," he said. The Mammoth Major was bought from an AEC enthusiast at Amersham, Bucks, and Ward found himself with a major project.

"It was a non-runner. The cab needed major work - there had even been a fire in it - and the chassis was cracked. That was just

the start," recalls Ward. The tank and cab were removed, as were the engine, gearbox and axles.

Chassis repairs were carried out by arc welding. The crossmember supporting the engine also needed major surgery. Otherwise the chassis was in what Ward describes as "reasonable nick" and responded well to shotblasting. The 9.6-litre AEC engine was really past saving. "The block and heads were cracked so I fitted an 11.3 litre unit, these being much more easily available," Ward said. The radiator was rebuilt with an extra set of tubes to cope with the increased engine capacity.

He had decided that it would be wise to try to increase the AEC's top speed, to make it much easier to use on the road. It will now do 45mph as opposed to 27 in the

spec when he got it.

The AEC gearbox was rebuilt, using some parts from another unit, and converted from five- to six-speed, no mean task. Higher ratio driving axles were fitted, and the tyres changed from 900x24s to original spec 900x20s. Ward recalls: "I scratched around and found a set of the proper wheels, three of which were off London Transport trolleybuses."

The cab needed a lot of attention. By law this had to be aluminium and steel-framed rather than wood-framed, because of the vehicle's use. Most of the steel was replaced during extensive upgrading. New doors were made, using the originals as patterns, and replacement outer and inner wings had to be fabricated.

The 3200 gallon tank was found to be in an extremely poor state but responded to

Cab extensively rebuilt - but looks original.

Ward has this Atkinson wrecker for sale to the right home.

patient welding! "No wonder people often take tanker bodies off lorries and put flats on instead," Ward mused. Attention to the manholes on top of the tanks was needed, along with new piping and catwalk, via which the driver gets on top of the tank.

A new wiring harness was needed and a replacement control box for the fire-damaged original. The driver and passenger seats had to be replaced, the new ones coming from an AEC Reliance bus and an Atkinson lorry.

Brakes were stripped completely and rebuilt with all parts being replaced. The correct spec lights were found, again contributing to the overall appearance.

Repainting was carried out by Ward, using photographs to recreate the original look. He used synthetic paint, then put on etch primer, two undercoats and two topcoats.

Signwriting was entrusted to David Carpenter, whose craft has been seen on buses for 35 years. The Royal Warrants on the side of the lorry were more difficult, being made up by a firm in Birmingham which specialises in producing these. Permission had to gained from Buckingham Palace to use these and the original pictures of the lorry sent as proof that the vehicle had this livery.

At last the AEC was finished, after, Ward says, 3200 hours' work, and a particularly fine addition to preservation's ranks took to the rally circuit. Not only will this AEC draw crowds for many years to come, but the EFE model will give pleasure and spread the classic commercial word in homes across the world.

Below: Tank needed a massive amount of work.

Havoline is still a well known name today.

WARD JONES COMMERCIALS is at Cryers Hill, High Wycombe, Bucks, tel 01494 711510.

AGAINST THE GRAIN

Paul Fox takes a look back at grain haulage in a golden era.

Photos: Paul Fox collection

The best of British in the LJ Lavender of Manea fleet, as shown in this picture from the firm's 1965 calendar.

The idea of flour milling evokes nostalgic images of windmills and water mills in sunny rural settings. It is as historic and basic as a loaf of bread. But of course it's a far cry from modern milling, which is a big industry and which in turn has been served by large fleets of lorries, run by big and small specialist hauliers.

Grain crops can be grown in various soils and Britain has many grain-growing areas and merchants. Early transport of grain from farm to mill was very much a job for strong men with broad shoulders, who often lifted hessian sacks weighing more than 2cwt, known as cumes.

Some of the earliest photos of milling show loads which have obviously been manhandled in sacks.

As manufacturers of tipping equipment developed bulk bodies and grain handling equipment was introduced, the handling of grain in bulk was established.

Many merchants chose a dropside body which allowed a vehicle to be used as a bulk tipper or for general carrying, as the merchants also supplied animal feed and fertilisers. The need for pallet loading as well as bulk carrying saw further developments in transport.

Some corn merchants used vehicles with bulk blowing devices which could discharge animal feed into bins and give bulk delivery with tailboard discharge.

For fixed side tippers in the 1950s and 60s, eight-wheelers were favoured by many, but the artic became more common from the 1970s onwards. At that time, many corn merchants ran their own vehicles but nowadays it's more common for corn marketing companies to use bulk haulage specialists.

Merchants were often family or privately-owned businesses, but as has been the case with other industries, many

Isons of Cambridge AECs. A Mercury with blower body and Mammoth Major platform.

Paul Fox's dad and elder brother load this L Lavender Albion bound for Spillers Silvertown.

Morris Commercial, Albion Chieftain and Gardner 4LW-powered Maudslay of L Lavender.

Sacks dated 1955 give away when this picture of a Guy Morton Commer, complete with sack loader, was taken. The Seddon seen inside the building has been immaculately restored by Tony Knowles.

have been absorbed into large farming co-operatives or multi-national companies.

The corn merchant usually offered drying facilities and storage, and was the middle man between farmer and miller.

In the Fenland area, for example, all flour millers were served, but a large amount was hauled to Spillers' Millennium Mill at Silvertown, London.

The names of Spillers, Ranks, Smiths, and Heygates would be common delivery names for corn merchant drivers, and all these operated large fleets themselves.

The Albion HD57 originally started as a platform vehicle and later received a Bonallack tipping body.

An interesting photo of sacks of grain being delivered on a platform is that of Guy Morton's Commer waiting outside a mill. He became one of the leading potato merchants in the country. His father's Seddon, seen loading at the mill, is now in Tony Knowles's immaculately restored preserved fleet.

The Commer also boasted a sack loader, which saved much heavy lifting when loading on a farm. The sacks are printed 1955, so we can tell when the photo was taken.

Greenwoods Transport was for many years one of the country's "big boys." Based at Ramsey, on the Fenland border, it often hauled agricultural products, and the photo here shows hessian sacks being loaded in a mill. The driver would take the sack off the chute at the rear of the lorry and "walk" each sack to the front.

Isons of Cambridge was a well-known corn merchant, and the AEC Mercury is

Typical of a handball load, as seen on this magnificent AEC Mammoth Major of Greenwoods Transport.

Brands of Witchford, near Ely, became Anglia Agricultural Merchants (AAM).

Three Albions at LJ Lavender's silos and drying facility at Manea.

fitted with a modern-for-its-day blower body, yet the Mammoth Major still has a platform.

Staying with AECs, Sid Billitt's Mercury NCE 250H is seen at his depot in the heart of the Fens. The dropside body could take bag deliveries if need be.

Below: Dennis Jubilant rarity in March.

Brands of Witchford, near Ely, became Anglia Agricultural Merchants (AAM) and with large storage facilities in ex-wartime Lancaster hangars could store thousands of tons of grain. The line-up of B-series

ERF and Guy Big Js makes a fine shot of the AAM fleet in the mid-70s.

However, many hauliers, particularly in the busy harvest period, employed hauliers, and Rayners Transport, Madingley, Cambs, was one of many wellknown bulk hauliers serving the industry. The Spanish Dodge R30 tractors were the mainstay of the fleet in the 70s. I have often thought what a nice contribution one of these would make to a classic rally, particularly with a sleeper cab.

Dade's Transport, Leverington, Cambs, operated the eight-wheel Volvo F86 on grain haulage. What I have often questioned is why this model, selling in its thousands, didn't normally have twin headlights.

Another wellknown name in grain handling was Healey Wilson, and the F86 survives as a yard shunter for a well-known Northamptonshire milling family.

I have some fond memories of this

Bedford S-type trio seen at March.

vehicle in its prime, when it was based at Streatham, Cambs. Once again, a fixed side tipping body was fitted.

LEW 740W was one of many lorries of the Clark and Butcher fleet based at Soham, Cambs. Leyland Clydesdale tractors were not that common and this company was one of the few flour milling firms in the area which brought in local grain. The platform trailer is loaded with some of the firm's bagged products, probably animal feeds, but the lorry could soon be hitched to the bulk tipper parked next to it for bulk deliveries.

Clark and Butcher also operated Albion LAD-cabbed tractors with the Scammell coupling. Over the years their vehicles could be seen in all aspects of grain related haulage as their first were powered by steam. The nostalgic street scene of a loaded six-wheel Dennis Jubilant was taken in Gaul Road, March, Cambs, outside the premises of Sid Billetts. Have any of these Jubilants survived?

The three Bedford S-types of Thomas Morton and Sons was taken at their yard and store in March. JJE 797 and KEB 259 had tipping bodies but KEB 258 was a platform. The firm's lorries would often have the legend "Stone Cross Feeds" on them, Stone Cross being an ancient monument in March.

The chains seen hanging on the left of the picture were a common method of hauling heavy sacks up to mills. The picture of three Albions was taken at LJ Lavender's silos and drying facility at Manea, Cambs. The four-wheel Chieftain offloads sacks while the eight wheel HD 57 and six-wheeler load from gravity feed shutes.

Like my previous contributions, these photos are only a peep into a large industry and I have only featured a few operators, Names which might also revive some

Quite a rarity in the Fens - a Leyland Clydesdale.

Volvo still exists as a yard shunter.

readers' memories include Hobbs of Ely, Satchells of Haddenham, Shelford Corn and Coal, Smarts of Whittlesford, Larretts of Chatteris and Somersham, and Huckles of Somersham.

Many deliveries of grain were made into London mills and often animal feed and feed ingredients were returned to the merchants, who then delivered to many Fenland farms.

A few more names - Charlie Brown of Vauxhall, Chelsea Flour Mills, Spillers, Rank, BOCM, CWS of Silvertown, Fullo Pep of Southall; Mark Mayhew and Sea Meal of Stratford. I'm sure readers could add many more names to the list.

THANKS
My thanks to everyone who loaned photos for this article.

Sid Billitt's AEC Mercury with dropside body capable of transporting bags of grain.

Below: The "Spanish" Dodge R30 tractors were the mainstay of the Rayners Transport fleet in the 70s.

CAFE SOCIETY!

Our series on great transport cafes continues with a Yorkshire concern that's not only still open, but thriving in changing times.

(Photos: Stan Wass/Stan Wass Collection)

For almost 70 years, lorry drivers have got out of their cabs and braved biting Pennine winds to enjoy the warmth and cosiness of the Motorman's Cafe, on the A62 at Marsden, near Huddersfield.

Originally run by members of the Haig and Dronsfield families, the Motorman's was taken over by the Woodwards in 1959. Doris Woodward and her daughter, Jean Hall, are the people behind the business today.

Older long distance lorry drivers will remember the 3-mile hill on which the cafe stands as 'Stanedge' though it's officially Standedge. The legendary Standedge railway tunnel is nearby.

In 1959, when the major photo in this feature was taken, there were two other nearby transport cafes, the Blue Peter, which has closed, and The Standedge Services, now a pub.

Anyone who even vaguely knows the area won't need reminding of the one development which very nearly finished off the Motorman's - the opening of the M62 in 1970.

"The A62 changed literally overnight from being a busy road to a virtually empty one. We had some very bad years, but we did have some faithful customers and a determination to keep going," said Jean.

Nowadays, customers have changed greatly, with tourists and general passers-by forming much of the clientele. Contractors working in the area are also among the customers.

There are also still the regulars. "We always love to see the older lorry drivers coming to pay us a visit. We got to know them so well over the years," said Jean.

The A62 was notorious for being blocked by snow during the severe winters of the post, so has the Motorman's regularly offered a home in the storm to stranded lorry drivers?

"People always ask that, but it hasn't been the case. When the snow's really bad here you can't see in front of you and I don't think many of the drivers would have managed to get to us".

Nowadays, families are welcome at the Motorman's. Added Jean: "We're not a Brewer's Fayre type of restaurant as far as catering for families is concerned but I think people like a traditional cafe such as this. That's how we intend to stay."

Drivers enjoying much needed sustenance in the early 1960s.

The Motorman's today, and in the 1960s.

Welcoming you – Jean Hall, about to serve up another cuppa!

A wonderful shot taken from the Motorman's car park, 1959. The Somnus bedding van and the Commer low-loader are heading west up Standedge, with 2 miles to go before reaching the top (wonder if the Commer, carrying that huge digger, got there before the M62 opened – Ed). The view remains virtually the same today – but the lorries have certainly changed!

MOTORMAN'S DETAILS
The Motorman's is on the A62, one mile west of Marsden, Huddersfield, tel 01484 844428.

Opening times:
Monday-Friday, 7.30am-2pm;
Sunday 9am-5pm.

Sample fare:
Roast beef dinner, £3.95,
Sunday roast dinner £4.95,
full breakfast £3.95, jam roly poly, £1.25.

The immaculate Borderer, a centrepiece of the Classic Atkinson Club's stand at our Donington show, turned out to be the result of a major restoration with much help from the club. Nick Larkin reports.

"Hmm, haven't seen this one before," thought I and many other people as we admired the immaculate Atkinson Borderer, WBF 543M, at the *Classic and Vintage Commercials* Donington event.

To be honest, though, the vehicle was shiny, yet it hadn't had a chance to shine, being confined to the relatively dark recesses of the Classic Atkinson Club's stand in the exhibition hall and surrounded by people. There were lots of other distractions, conversations, other vehicles, things to buy and, of course, attention was diverted in the frenzied anticipation of attending the prestigious Meet the Editors event at the show. Err, possibly.

It was only when the Atki emerged into the sunlight at the end of the day that its true colours were shown. Finally there was a chance to talk to the owner, Warwickshire haulier Garry George, and discover just how much work had gone into this vehicle. A frightening amount, in fact.

Garry has run his Grendon-based business for eight years, running Scanias and MANs.

But something was missing: "I've always wanted something old, and when I saw the Atkinson, it fitted the bill."

WBF 543M, a 1973 Borderer with Cummins 240 engine, is believed to

Haulier Garry George had always wanted an old lorry to restore.

have been new to Samuel Johnston of Burton upon Trent. Garry has connections with the Staffordshire town, having trained as a mechanic with local firm Translitre. Neither Garry or the Atki were destined to spend their entire working lives in Burton, the lorry heading to Pilkington Bros in County Durham. It finished up with Keeling of Weston-Super-Mare, from whom Garry bought it.

First impressions were of a reasonably sound machine which ran well. But then came the disasters.

"When we took the front corner panel off, things started escalating. There was a bit of wood which needed replacing here and a bit there. Then another bit and another bit.

"In the end, major work was carried out on the cabframe, including the complete replacement of the nearside corner pillar."

But there was a stroke of luck. The Classic Atkinson Club managed to source all the woodwork to complete the task in original-specification ash. "I don't know what I would have done otherwise," said Garry, "but it took quite a bit of effort to get everything back together."

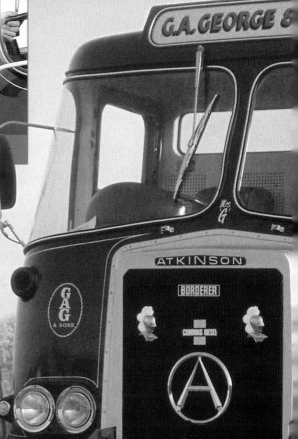

(All photos: Nick Larkin)

CTIVATED

Definitely no hope of getting away with vinyls here. Traditional signwriting was the only option!

Fibreglass panels were re-used before a superb respray carried out in two-pack.

Upholstery and cab fittings had survived in remarkably good condition.

Complete! Atkinson Borderer tractor unit after its major restoration.

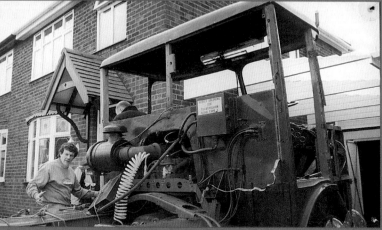

(Restoration photos: Garry George)

Panels removed to find horrors. Work on the door is taking place here.

Cab stripped and new woodwork fitted prior to replacement aluminium rear panelwork being restored.

Before painting usable, saving

Lorry hides the amount of work carried out to the rear of the cab.

The floor had also rotted out, this being made from steel – four pieces on the driver's side and two on the passenger side. New sections were made up, using the originals as patterns.

There was more rot to deal with. The cab back panel, a notorious Borderer rot spot, had to be replaced. Originally made from steel, Garry, like several other Borderer restorers before him, opted for a replacement in aluminium, again sourced with club help.

The cab doors had to be rebuilt. "The only bit that's original on the doors is the glass and the doorskins," he said.

Once again, it was club help to the rescue, with channels and other parts supplied. Due to the complexities of the door woodwork, Garry entrusted this to carpenter FW Grace of Tamworth, Staffordshire.

Better news was that all the Atki's glassfibre panels were, with a bit of work, reusable. The cab fittings including the upholstery had, unlike all around them, survived well, though the door trims needed to be replaced, as did the window rubbers.

"The interior was so original that if you'd started replacing bits, it just wouldn't have looked like an old lorry, or looked right."

The chassis had quite a bit of surface rust, but responded well to shotblasting. Repainting the vehicle was entrusted to K-Spray of Lutterworth, Leics, and the result, carried out in two-pack, is excellent.

Signwriting was carried out by Barrie Eaton, whose work is to be seen on Garry's modern vehicles. "Obviously he couldn't do it in vinyls, so he had to get his brushes out to do the job in traditional style. I'm really pleased with how it turned out," said Garry.

The brakes. Ah yes, the brakes. Despite

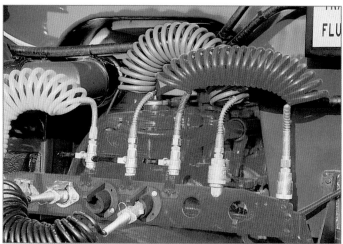

Cummins 240 engine needed little work. 'Suzies' were replaced.

Replacement fifth wheel proved relatively easy to fit.

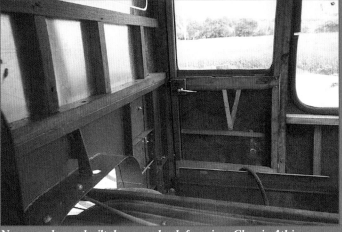

...ss panels were re-
...me.

New wood on rebuilt doors and cab framing. Classic Atkinson Club proved a major help here.

Chassis suffered from surface rust, but responded well to shotblasting.

all his mechanical experience, Garry was foxed.

"I did think that little would be needed apart from freeing off, cleaning and checking, but I was wrong. The brakes just kept locking up when the wheels turned. Eventually I managed to get hold of an Atkinson Borderer workshop manual. I had a terrible time with it."

A noticeable feature of the Atki was that it was leaning to one side. "I assumed it was a weak spring, so thought I might as well replace them on both sides – end of problem and hopefully of uneven spring wear."

The Atkinson's fifth wheel had been removed, and Garry decided to replace it. A replacement came from well-known Redditch-based restorer Gary Hughes.

"The new fifth wheel wasn't too difficult to put on. A little bit of modification on the flitch plates so it went over the spring hangers and dropped straight on, being bolted onto the flitch plates."

The wooden 'catwalk' across the chassis was restored to original specification.

"It cost me a fortune as it's proper mahogany, but I felt it was worth the extra. It just looks right."

Engine-wise, there were few problems apart from work being needed on the compressor. A thorough service was required, as you'd expect. Added Garry: "The radiator was out when I bought the lorry, and I decided that instead of trying to put the old one back in, when major repairs might be needed, I'd buy a new one."

Cab mountings all had to be changed, with new latches being put on. The electrics were a bit of a mess, so major remedial work was carried out by Garry

himself. The 'Suzies' were also renewed.

He had reservations about one of the Atki's concessions to comfort – its power steering.

"I didn't really want power steering, but I thought that as it was there, I didn't want to take it off. The system was in good condition anyway."

And so that was it, the completion of Garry's first restoration project.

"I'd always wanted to do up a truck, and I think this one will do for now. There was more to do with this vehicle than I thought, but I don't mind when it's a lorry like this!"

THANKS
Garry would like to thank the Classic Atkinson Club for all its help with the restoration. Details of the club, which caters for all Atkis, on 01590 675701.

GARRY'S TIPS FOR RESTORERS

Make sure you know what you're doing. Get a workshop manual and study it.

Look into potential jobs in some depth. Find out exactly what's needed to be done, and the parts which will be needed.

FINE

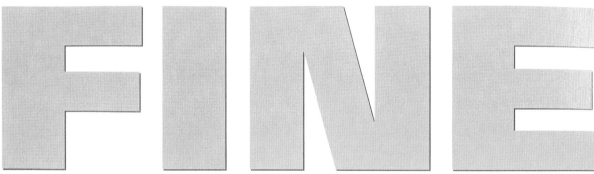

*More retail nostalgia as we look at Fine Fare's lorries –
including a unique restored ERF – and take a quick sneak at
J Sainsbury. Nick Larkin reports.*

"**W**here you can be fair to your family, and your purse!' The once well-known slogan of late-lamented supermarket chain, Fine Fare. You might even remember Scottish actor Gordon Jackson preaching it in television commercials during the bleak early 1980s. He used the same tone of voice as when he admonished Rose in Upstairs Downstairs.**

You could see the advertising moguls' reasoning for choosing Mr Jackson. Mature man from telly, a Scot, therefore stingy – sorry, someone careful but frugal. It must be true, if he, Gordon, tells us so. Alvin Stardust just wouldn't have had the same impact.

Fine Fare, despite being a highly successful household name, disappeared 15 years or so ago, gulped up by Dee Corporation. Yet the name is being kept alive by a superbly restored 1982 ERF C40, carefully looked after by its owner of 10 years, Anthony Perry, whose dad drove the lorry in service. More on that later.

The Fine Fare brand originated in Canada, but the UK operation was part of Associated British Foods, owned by entrepreneur Garfield Weston. The company expanded rapidly during the 1960s, taking over several well-known grocery chains such as Melias along with regional operations such as Waterworth Bros and WM Cussons.

By the early 1970s, Fine Fare was a highly respected national name, even running some High Street Fine Fare Coffee Bars. The chain managed to cultivate a slightly upmarket image: "Nice stores for nice people," as one commentator said. In less leafy areas, Shoppers' Paradise stores opened with their trademark cheap and frill-free character.

Fine Fare's orange lorries were soon seen everywhere, the company being a major ERF customer. In the 1980s, it was decided to modernise the fleet image and so a changeover to blue began, though this was quashed when the Dee Corporation took over Fine Fare and quickly imposed its Gateway brand.

Fine Fare had a tremendous following in Scotland where it sponsored the Scottish Football League. Thus the name survived

(Photo: Nick Larkin)

*After looking at this .
hours, we worked ou*

It was my dad's truck. Anthony Perry with ERF.

(Photo: David Reed)

*Restored – and very orange – family
heirloom. ERF C-series is now 20 years old.*

118

FARE!

BEERS, WINES, SPIRITS, FROZEN AT PRE-BUDGET PRICES.

CASH-IN

FINE FARE SUPERSTORES & SUPERMARKETS
Where you can be fair to your family, and your purse

logo for several
rised two Fs!

(Photo: Nick Larkin)

Look at the bargains! Fine Fare newspaper ad, 1980.

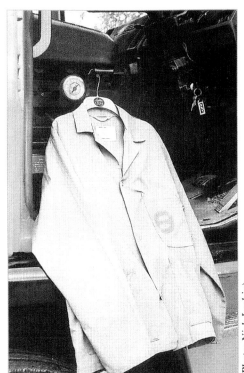

(Photo: Nick Larkin)

Would you wear a Fine Fare jacket for a photoshoot? Anthony reckons it's too small for him. Any excuse!

(Photo: Nick Larkin)

(Photo: Nick Larkin)

New rear wings fitted during restoration.

(Photo: Nick Larkin)

Cab fittings survived in good condition.

longer there, with lorries that had been painted in the new colours often being transferred to Scotland in exchange for orange ones which would then be 'Gateway-ised'.

A FAMILY CONNECTION

Fine Fare's 'family and purse' slogan certainly rings true as far as the restoration of a unique ERF C-series is concerned. EUR 316Y was driven from new by Malcolm Perry, father of present owner and restorer Anthony. As for the 'purse' – well, change that to 'wallet' because Anthony's carried out a budget restoration of the ERF over the 10 years he's owned it.

Mr Perry senior worked at Fine Fare's Hucknall (Nottingham) depot when he was allocated the bright orange ERF. He'd started his career as a van driver with

Burtons of Smithy Row in Nottingham, a regional grocers taken over by Fine Fare in the early 1960s.

Son Anthony, who remembers travelling in the lorry as a lad, said: "My love affair with lorries began when I first went out with my dad in his lorry at the age of five… and every school holiday after that."

The first regular steed was a Cummins V8-engined Ford D Series, OAR 410H. "As a five year old, the noise of the fridge motor used to frighten me, though I'd love to know what happened to this vehicle," he said.

The Ford's replacement was Leyland Buffalo PNG 856R, which had been a demonstrator with Mann Egerton of Norwich. Buffalos were extensively used by Fine Fare at the time – but over the years, Lynx and Marathons were also operated.

So were ERFs from KV to LV and E-Series, not forgetting Volvo F7s, Scania 92 and 112s, with rigids including Dodge Commandos and Leyland Clydesdales. As well as Hucknall, Fine Fare had depots at Aylesford, Manchester, Gloucester, Washington, Weedon and East Kilbride.

Finally, both father and son were delighted when ERF EUR 316Y arrived. An ERF C402RT, it was unique among Fine Fare's ERFs in being a C40 model fitted with a Rolls-Royce 290L Eagle Engine, a Fuller Roadranger gearbox and a Rockwell rear axle – the others having the 265L engine and Kirkstall axle. Why this was the case, no one knows.

EUR entered service on store deliveries and was allocated fleet number 9, though this practice was dropped in 1983-84.

When the vehicle was a year old, it was

FINE FARE NOSTALGIA

(Photos: Anthony Perry)

(Photo: Ted Short)

Bedford artics were extensively used in the 1960s. This is a TK, 2374 NK, along with step-frame trailer.

Leyland Buffalos were popular with Fine Fare in the 1970s. This pair were shunters at Hucknall depot in 1987.

EUR 318Y was a Seddon Atkinson, seen at Gloucester. It sports the new blue and white livery for trailers.

Best in the long run

Goodyear put more money into research and development than any other tyre manufacturer in the world. The G291 is positive proof this investment pays off.

A high technology, steel radial tyre that leaves other long distance runners way behind.

Look how the advantages add up. An even wearing, high mileage tyre giving positive steering control and excellent resistance to wet skid. Plus greatly reduced running temperatures. Like all other tyres in the G series, the advanced casing construction provides the big bonus of superb remouldability.

A casing highly acclaimed by all leading retreaders.

All round, the Goodyear G291 is the most cost effective long distance tyre on the road.

And, it is a direct result of our planned programme to bring you the best tyre technology in the world. The Goodyear G291 is now also available in 75 and 80 series.

So fit the world's best all round truck tyre, because the investment we've put behind it will pay off for you in the future.

G291 THE WORLD'S BEST ALL ROUND TRUCK TYRE

"I find Goodyear G291 cost effective, a good steering tyre, with the bonus of good casings for remould."
S. McBRIDE Group Transport Manager Fine Fare

THE WORLD LEADERS IN TYRE TECHNOLOGY

GOODYEAR

Ignore the registration number. This is EUR 316Y starring in the 1984 Goodyear advertisement. If you look closely at the full-sized original, you can see Malcolm Perry's British Rail totem sticker on the rear bulkhead. He used to work on steam locomotives.

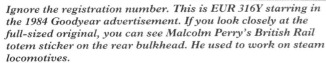

(Photo: Nick Larkin)

Malcolm Perry at the wheel of the ERF in its service days.

cleaned and hitched to a brand new trailer for a starring role – in an advertisement for Goodyear G291 tyres, which appeared in numerous truck magazines, the lorry receiving an A-registration for the part. Its 15 minutes of fame over, EUR settled down to a normal life.

Fine Fare had been pioneers of curtainside trailers. The Hucknall depot tended to use step-frame single-axle trailers, progressing to straight box vans with barn doors at 24ft long, then 26ft axles and roller shutter doors, finally 32 ton tandem axle up to 40ft maximum length. Makes used included Crane Fruehauf, York and Craven Tasker. Lorries were generally single shifted, unlike the double

and even treble shifting that's the norm today.

In mid-1986, EUR was painted into Gateway green and yellow, then in 1987, the Hucknall operations were taken over by BRS (Midlands) Ltd. There were many redundancies and though the ERF was kept, Malcolm Perry wasn't – he's now a driver with Nottingham City Transport.

EUR 316Y was finally withdrawn in June 1989, then being sold by Cossington Commercials via an auction at Manchester. It then passed to Blurton Transport Services of Stoke-on-Trent. It was uprated from 32 to 38 tonnes, given tipping gear and used on bulk haulage. Due to lack of work, it was later used on local shunting

and towing jobs with trade plates.

Meanwhile, all those journeys with his dad, and some work experience in Hucknall, had instilled a determination in Anthony to enter the road transport industry. After his O-levels, he started work as a YTS traffic clerk at Joseph Merritt and Son Ltd, a machinery removals company. He then worked at AET Transport, K&M Hauliers of Hucknall and from 1995, Hays Distribution. In 1998, he won the Transport and Distribution Manager of the Year Award.

It was during a discussion with colleagues that the subject of EUR 316Y came up. Why didn't Anthony try to find it? And so he did – all the way to Blurton

WBH 787X, seen at Hucknall, has the blue livery meant to modernise the orange, which soon disappeared following the Dee Corporation takeover.

(Photo: Anthony Perry)

Shoppers' Paradise was Fine Fare's no-frills subsidiary, which tended to have shops in less leafy areas.

(Photo: Anthony Perry)

Gateway days, and this DAF 2500 shows off the full livery. Gateway has disappeared after being re-titled Somerfield.

Engine needed little attention during restoration, but cooling fan was renewed.

Bumper stove was enamelled and some re-fibreglassing carried out.

Transport. Armed with a camera, Anthony went to have a look.

"I'd no intention of buying it. I just wanted to have a look for old time's sake," he insists. "While chatting to the owner, it was revealed that the lorry was only used as a shunter, and would be available. I found myself making an offer."

A check by mechanic friend, Neil Utting, confirmed the ERF was in excellent condition, so money changed hands and EUR 316Y was driven back to undercover storage in Nottinghamshire.

That was in 1993, and not much was done apart from keeping it in running order, changing the antifreeze and painting the chassis.

Then in 2000, circumstances changed. "I found myself young, free and single, and it seemed the ideal opportunity to crack on and finish the truck. On the horizon was the ERF/REVS Coming Home, Moving Home event, which was an extra incentive."

BJJ trucks near Elford, Tamworth, had a large collection of old/dismantled ERFs in their yard, which produced many useful spares.

"I soon discovered what an all-consuming task restoration can be – especially when you have little practical knowledge of mechanics and are working on your own," he remembers. "That said, the work would never have been done without the priceless help and advice given by many colleagues and friends."

Working to a strict deadline with a full-time job and social life was a tall order, never mind Anthony's other hobby…

(Photo: Anthony Perry)

A young Anthony with the ERF in October 1985. The location is Beverley, East Yorks.

(Photo: Anthony Perry)

EUR 316Y in a freezing Yarmouth lorry park in the winter of 1982/3.

(Photo: Anthony Perry)

Back on the road but not repainted. ERF in Blurton Transport livery.

playing the tuba in a brass band!

But that did not stop him. First, evidence of accident damage around the nearside step and wing was dealt with by re-fibreglassing. New rear wings and mudflaps were fitted. The fuel injection pump was overhauled and a new secondary filter fitted. The radiator and hoses were also replaced, the front bumper stove enamelled.

Also renewed was the cab tilt pump and pipes, which he found surprisingly to be a relatively straightforward job. New shock absorbers, flasher unit and catwalk were all fitted.

The cab was finally stripped of paint. "Sometimes it seemed I was taking two steps forward and three back," said Anthony. "I was flogging day in, day out, with a small scraper before discovering the benefits of hand drills and Nitromors."

Before he knew it, it was time for an MoT – which the ERF passed first time – and the Banbury Steam Rally. It appeared in a roadworthy but cosmetically unappealing state as the repaint had yet to be carried out. When done, the Fine Fare orange transformed the lorry.

"A phone call to Masons led me to a gentleman in the colour labs who knew the Fine Fare paint codes off the top of his head," says Anthony. Classic Signs and Lines of Mansfield made up the Fine Fare logo and lettering, working from photos.

New keys came easily – local ERF dealer Toptrux in Nottingham was able to get them from the vehicle's chassis number. C40 badges were also supplied.

Now the ERF attracts a lot of attention. "Obviously ERF enthusiasts look at it as a good example of an early 1980s' C-series, but many people find it fascinating in its Fine Fare guise. It was something you saw every day, but has now gone." Anthony is now hoping, storage permitting, to get an original Fine Fare Crane Freuhauf trailer to complete the combination.

Needless to say, Anthony's dad is delighted at his son's achievement. Anthony says: "I've tried to restore it as authentically as possible, though lack of spares and finance has led to one or two non-standard fittings. Now the lorry's looking good, recalling both my childhood and my dad's past. It's a real family heirloom."

EUR 316Y and some sister vehicles just after being painted in Gateway colours.

THANKS

Many thanks to Anthony for supplying many of the photos and much information for this feature. Anthony would like to thank his partner Ann, his dad, friend Neil Utting, East Midlands Commercials, Rob Bradbury, PB Auto Electrics, Toptrux, REVs, BJJ Trucks, Eurotrucks, Masons Paints, Jeyes Engineering supplies and everyone else who helped in one way or another with the restoration.

SAINSBURY ATKI

We're not going to say too much about this former Sainsbury's Atkinson Borderer because we hope to feature its full restoration in a future issue, along with that of Atki owner Clive MacDonald's extraordinary S&D dustcart. But here's a sneak preview.

PJD 817L, a T3046LX model, was first registered in May 1973 as a short wheelbase 30-ton tractor unit, fitted with a Gardner 150LX engine, David Brown six-speed gearbox and Kirkstall 5.75 ratio rear axle.

Supplied to Sainsbury by Atkinson Vehicles (London) Ltd, it had extra equipment fitted to the supermarket's specification – full power steering, Bostram seats and a hydraulic pump to gearbox PTO to run a Bonallack 30ft single axle Concorde fridge trailer.

The Atki was allocated to Buntingford (Herts) depot, servicing stores in the Birmingham and Coventry area – running two shifts totalling 20 hours a day.

Sold to the McKewen Bros, boxing booth showmen of Collumpton, Devon, the fifth wheel was removed, the chassis extended by three feet and a box body fitted with a generator.

After passing through several other owners, the Atki ended up with Clive MacDonald of Surrey in 1996. Clive has removed the box body, returned the chassis to its original length, rebuilt the engine and removed and reframed the cab – a 17-month restoration.

(Photo: Nick Larkin)

Ex-Sainsbury's Atkinson Borderer, as exhibited at this year's Bromley Pageant of Motoring.

SALES PITCHES

Could this be why the British lorry industry declined? In 1965, a major new company approached several manufacturers about an order for at least 150 vehicles. The lorry makers' responses have survived, and the attitude of some is astonishingly apathetic and inflexible. Richard Mellor takes up the story.

When OCL was formed by four long-established British shipping companies in 1965, it approached all the major vehicle manufacturers about buying a fleet of 150 to 200 tractor units.

These would be operated from depots in strategic demand locations in Britain and Europe. There were some interesting presentations and quotations to OCL, and some of the sales managers, of whom one would have thought better, made some very half-hearted sales pitches for what one would have thought would have been attractive business.

This was especially so considering that they would be getting in at the start of a new transport concept which could only grow. The submissions from manufacturers have survived and make interesting reading 40 years later, when the cream of the world's vehicle manufacturers exist no longer.

AEC

AEC, with its historic "Vangastow" telegraphic address, offered the Mandator TG4R, allowing a gross train weight of 30 tons, and the 6x2 twin steer Mammoth Minor TG6RF, with 32 tons gtw, permissible with a three-axle tractor since 1964.

AEC's Mammoth Minor twin-steer tractor was suited to tandem axle trailers for 32-ton operation under the original 13m length limit. (Photo: Peter Davies)

The time quoted for delivery was 18 months from receipt of order. Apart from the Ergomatic tilt cab (see below), offering 'saloon car comfort and styling, with modern safety standards and superb engine accessibility', the Mandator featured either an AEC AV 691 six-cylinder (dry liners) diesel, developing up to 205 bhp at 2200 rpm, or the more powerful 225 bhp AV760, both with nitride hardened counterbalanced crankshaft, six-speed overdrive gearbox, single dry plate clutch, and double reduction spiral bevel final drive.

A 75-gallon fuel tank was fitted, there were leaf springs with telescopic, direct-acting hydraulic dampers on the front axle, and 24-volt electrical system.

The AV 691 had a bore of 5.12 in and stroke of 5.59 in, giving a capacity of 690 cu in (as hinted by the type designation), just over 11 litres, with maximum torque 573 lb ft at 1200 rpm. The AV760 had a bore of 5.38 in and stroke of 5.59 in, giving a capacity of 761 cu in (12.25 litres), with maximum torque 618 lb ft at 1500 rpm.

Overall length of the tractor was 16ft 9 1/2 in on a 9ft. 6in wheelbase, and an excellent turning circle, 41ft (the Foden equivalent was 66ft). Steering was the worm and nut variety, requiring 6.75 turns from lock to lock.

ATKINSON

Atkinson Vehicles, of Preston, was keen to sell its Silver Knight T3046C model, with Cummins NHE 180 six-cylinder oil engine, giving 173 bhp at 1950 rpm, ZF AK.6-7.5 gearbox, Kirkstall double helical double reduction axle, and a 54-gallon fuel tank. The quoted price was £3642 5s, plus a small delivery charge to a location in the south of England.

Interestingly, the quotation was made by the London sales office, off Nightingale Lane, SW12, reminding us of the connections with its 1933 rescuer, WG Allen FCA, and his family business, Nightingale Engineering.

AEC Mandator featured the Sankey-built Ergomatic cab and a choice of AV691 or AV760 engines with power outputs of 205 and 225bhp. (Photo: Peter Davies)

Above: Atkinson Silver Knight tractor with Mk1 glass fibre cab had a choice of Gardner 150, Cummins NHE180 or NH220 engines. (Photo: Peter Davies)

ERF

E Sherratt, a director of ERF, offered a 15-month lead time to production of the first vehicle (Yes, you read that right, 15 months for the FIRST vehicle - Ed), then 14 months for delivering 150 of its 64CU180 four-wheel tractor, operating at 30 tons gvw.

He stressed the strength and rigidity of the glass fibre panels on the wood and steel framework of the LV cab, describing it also as comfortable(!) and business-like, with no maintenance requirements. The standard three-line braking system was emphasised also.

FODEN

In contrast, Mr D Foden presented the details of twin (AE6/28) and tri-axle (DF AE6/32) Foden tractors. One could buy glass fibre cabbed units, with the FD6 Mk VI oil engine, developing 175 bhp at 2200 rpm and with a 12-speed gearbox, or at no extra cost, the Leyland P680, developing an extra 25 bhp. The Cummins NH220 engine was quoted as £363 more expensive. A 15 per cent discount for an order of 200 vehicles was available and the lead time for delivery of the first two vehicles was 20 months.

GUY

Guy Motors put forward the Big J 4T for operation at 30 or 32 tons, with 12 to 18 months for delivery, and the Invincible Mk III. The Big J 4T, with six-speed overdrive constant mesh

Foden could offer a tilt cab, the S24, on its tractor, which was powered by a Foden FD6 Mk VI two-stroke diesel developing 175bhp. (Photo: Peter Davies)

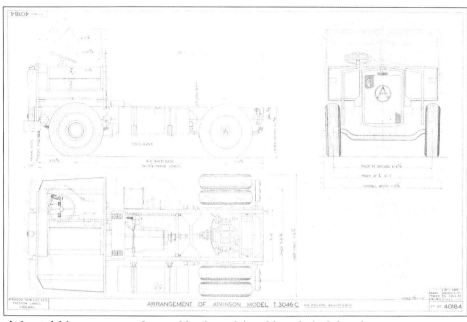

At least Atkinson went to the trouble of supplying this technical drawing.

gearbox and Gardner 6LX engine developing 150 bhp at 1700 rpm, was proposed.

The cab was all-steel welded construction, main access to the engine was through the inside of the cab but the cab be tilted by a mechanical jack for major engine overhaul or removal. Overall length of the unit was 14 ft 11 in.

Being part of Jaguar Cars, Guy publicised the Big J accompanied by a Jaguar E type - quality and performance was the message.

The Invincible, described by Guy Motors as rugged, robust and reliable, was offered to OCL with the Gardner 6LX diesel engine and David Brown six-speed constant mesh gearbox. The cab assembly was in two sections, the top made of a highly durable reinforced plastic, and the assembly below the waistline being an all steel structure, weather sealed on the underside. The excellent visibility from the cab was stressed, provided by the wrap-round panoramic windscreen in toughened plate glass.

LEYLAND

Leyland Motors offered to supply 100 units from the Beaver Freightline range, of model 14BT/17R, with the 0680 Mk II diesel engine (usually available then only in left-hand drive models), with an expected life of the vehicle quoted as 10 to 15 years and delivery starting 24 months after receipt of order.

The accompanying brochure, however, made no mention of this model! Features included the engine producing 200 bhp at 2200 rpm. The 0680 engine had a 5in bore and 5.75 in stroke, giving a capacity of 677 cu in or nearly 11 litres. Maximum torque was 548 lb ft at 1200 rpm on a compression ratio of 15.8:1. Fuel consumption was quoted as 0.395 lb/bhp/hr, but only a 48-gallon fuel tank was provided.

A six-speed overdrive gearbox, power

ERF 64CU tractor has a choice of Cummins 180 or 220 and features the 6LV glass fibre cab. (Photo: Peter Davies)

assisted steering and handbrake and the all-steel Ergomatic tilt cab (55 degrees) were fitted. In describing the cab, Leyland rightly emphasised it being the "result of intensive development arising from an extensive ergonomic study of the driving function carried out by Leyland engineers under worldwide operating conditions." Also stressed, among other things, were the safety aspects derived from the cab's "massive double skin steel crash protection" and a "windscreen giving superb visibility". Other claims were that the "Luxurious trim promoted comfort and alertness".

OK, it was not up to modern standards but in the mid-1960s, it was innovative, a major step forward in the area of previously ignored driver comfort and way ahead of its rivals.

Which would you prefer - a comparatively comfortable Leyland rubber-mounted shock absorbent cab, with adjustable seats to accommodate you whatever your size, and a good heating/demisting system, or the spartan, noisy conditions provided for you by Guy or Atkinson? I know my choice at the time!

If further development of the Beaver range (and the AEC Mandator) had been properly funded, Leyland might have produced world-beating designs and still be with us. Unfortunately, employees have no option but to put their faith in their management and in Leyland's case, it was repaid by a kick in the teeth.

Leyland also offered a tilt cab - the Sankey-built Ergomatic as seen on this Freightline Beaver with a Power-Plus O.680 delivering 200bhp. (Photo: Peter Davies)

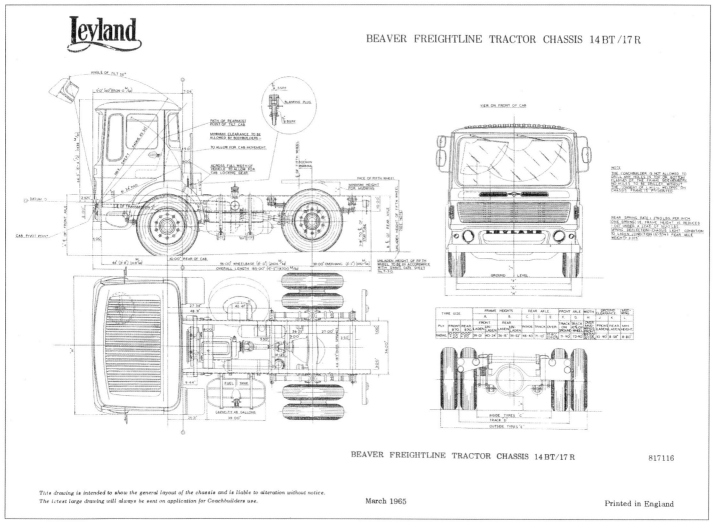

The Beaver Freightline, Leyland's candidate for OCL's business, certainly looked good on paper!

DASHED FOREIGNERS 1 - MAGIRUS

Of the two foreign presentations, the first was by Klockner-Humboldt-Deutz AG, of Ulm, Germany, which had only introduced its vehicles to Britain in 1965.

The manufacturing business had been started in 1864 by Conrad Magirus, originally building fire-fighting equipment. It was merged later with what had been the world's first factory for the manufacture of petrol engines, founded in the Deutz suburb of Cologne by Nikolaus "four stroke cycle" Otto and Eugen Langen. Interestingly, the Magirus badge represented the shape of Ulm Cathedral, which with its 528ft high spire, when viewed from one angle, suggested an elongated letter M. Its products were offered with air-cooled diesel engines, which KHD marketed as having the benefits of a reduction in potential breakdowns by eliminating radiators, water pumps, gaskets and hoses. Other selling points were "luxurious cabs, tried and tested braking systems', with an exhaust brake to help improve brake lining life; and speed of maintenance, all combining to give a "long economic life and efficient operation".

The Magirus 210D16FS model was offered, with V6 air-cooled Deutz four-stroke direct injection diesel, giving 150 bhp at 2300 rpm and with maximum torque of 383.35 ft lb at 1300 rpm. The cooling system was controlled by a hydraulically-operated axial blower to maintain a constant engine operating temperature whatever the season.

2 - DAF

The final quotation from Van Doorne's Automobielfabriek nv, of Eindhoven (DAF), Netherlands, was for 150 vehicles, with delivery starting only three months after placing an order.

The model suggested was the series 1800 DS, with a RS 576 six-cylinder ohv direct injection turbocharged diesel engine giving165hp at 2400 rpm. The unit cost was less than that of the British manufacturers, even allowing for delivery from the Netherlands, with the quotation innovatively combining an offer to supply the trailers as well. DAF's helpful sales department claimed that it was the only tractor manufacturer which could supply semi-trailers also, but this was not strictly true because Scammell could do the same and Foden seemed quite closely linked to Crane Fruehauf. Scammell did quote OCL for supplying skeletal trailers but not a package involving the complete rig.

It demonstrated how Leyland's former pupils and customers were coming up on the inside track, later to become the conquerors - the foreigners were well on their way to getting a foot in the door, giving the British manufacturers the icy draught of European competition, and wisely, they were offering an attractive package which differentiated their product from their English counterparts.

The competitive ex-works pricing position (£) of maximum gvw tractors, before fleet discount (about 15 per cent at that time), looked as follows:-

Company	2 axle tractor
AEC	3575
Atkinson	3642
Foden	4443
Leyland	3720
DAF	3065

All the British manufacturers, except Guy, had London sales offices with fashionable addresses, which seemed extravagant in retrospect, in view of their financial positions. However, this was before the big influx of Continental vehicles and the long waiting times from order to delivery told a story in itself about the demand and supply position in the commercial vehicle manufacturing industry.

Unladen weights were important when assessing potential payloads of competing products and as examples, kerb weights compared as follows:-

AEC Mandator TG4R	5 tons 1 cwt 3 qtr
Foden AE 6/28	4 tons 13 cwt 3 qtr
Leyland Beaver	5 tons 13 cwt
DAF 1800 DS	4 tons 10 cwt 3 qtr
Guy Invincible III	3 tons 15 cwt 3 qtr

Despite all this flurry of activity obtaining quotes for the supply of vehicles, in the end it was decided not to acquire any at all, but buy skeletal trailers instead. A mixture of contract hire vehicles would be used to cover the basic requirements, and spot hired vehicles would be brought in when necessary to cover peaks in demand.

The Guy Big J4T with Motor Panels cab had Cummins as its leading engine choice. (Photo: Peter Davies)

An extremely attractive package from Holland - available much more quickly than British alternatives. This DAF T1800 tractor unit was powered by the 575DS turbocharged diesel - a development of the Leyland Comet O.350. (Photo: Peter Davies)

TRANSCONTINENTALS STILL CHARMING

A recovery firm has what is believed to be the country's largest fleet of working Ford Transcontinentals. We pay a visit to learn more.

Gyles Carpenter took the photos.

Still in use in the Translink Recovery fleet is this 1978 Ford Transcontinental seen on the cover of a Ford brochure when new in the livery of London-based John Whelpley Ltd.

No one wants their lorry to break down but for those who do run into difficulty, especially classic truck enthusiasts, there could well be a pleasant surprise if Translink Recovery comes to your rescue.

SMF 911S remains an artic and is used to take trailers away from accidents as well as yard work.

This Lympne, Kent, fleet runs five lovingly kept Ford Transcontinentals - 23 years after the last examples were built. They're used every day over a wide area in Britain and sometimes abroad, and Translink intends to keep the survivors in service for as long as possible. They're part of a widely varying 42-strong fleet ranging from Volvo FH16 to Mercedes Varios.

The Transcontinental was Ford's competent contender in the 44-ton market. Using a modified Berliet cab, Cummins engines and Fuller gearboxes, the model was introduced in 1975. The lorries were built at the Amsterdam plant except the last 500 or so, production being switched to the unlikely location of the Foden factory at Elworth, Sandbach, Cheshire, by then owned by Paccar. The last examples left there in 1982.

Translink Recovery was founded 14 years ago by Andy Smith, who had a driving career before working for a Volvo agent and another recovery company.

Operations Manager Paul Bailey also favours the Transcontinentals. "They were over-engineered," he says, "and the chassis were made of high tensile steel, as anyone who's tried to drill through one will tell you. It's virtually impossible."

The lorries were built substantially from component parts, and generally spares are not too hard to find. "It was said in their day that the only thing Ford made on these lorries was the profit," commented Paul. One or two spares are difficult to get. The cabs, obviously, but also some brake valves and particularly the cable-operated foot valves - and the cables for them.

Translink (Paul assures us the firm didn't take the 'Trans' part of its name from the Fords) has done a lot of work on various examples it's had over the years. "We've changed engines and cabs - in fact what haven't we done?" says Paul. The

Beast of the fleet, Q849 NPP (centre) apparently knocks spots off the Volvo F16 standing next to it!

Left and above: Cab laid out to high standard, which many say set the trend leading to today's trucks.

lorries have proved highly reliable though: "I wouldn't hesitate sending one anywhere." Paul particularly praises the Transcon cab: "This was particularly advanced - I think it's the reason why trucks are as they are today," he said,

The Translink examples all have 14-litre engines, some having the four-cam version of the Cummins.

One star of the fleet is definitely the 1978 tractor SMF 911S, which was featured new on the cover of a Ford brochure in the livery of London-based haulier and remover John Whelpley Ltd. The backdrop to the picture is presumably Docklands.

Said Paul: "We don't know how the photo came about, but we were amazed to see it. A man came in who had picked up a load of lorry literature at a boot sale and said, 'I know you like these old Fords, and I found this old brochure.'

Different crane and winch specifications mean Transcons can tackle a wide range of jobs.

129

Oldest (and relatively most lethargic!) Transcon in the fleet is this 1975 example.

One of the last Transcontinentals built (at Foden Sandbach works!) A601 LKR was new to Indesit.

Then it twigged that the lorry on the front was ours."

Bought in Kent in April 1999, SMF 911S is used for hauling trailers back from breakdowns and general yard work.

Oldest example in the fleet is JAR 54N, a Mk I Transcontinental bought in 2001. This has a Holmes 750 crane fitted for underlift. "It only has the small cam motor and is a bit asthmatic, though once it gets going its all right. We've had a full weight artic on it without problems," said Paul.

Undoubted heavyweight of the line-up is Q849 NPP, bought in 1998. One of two built for Godfrey Davis, this beast has been a recovery vehicle from new and boasts a Wreckers International crane, heavy duty axle, a 370 Big Cam Cummins and 13-speed Fuller gearbox. "It will easily outpull our FH16," said Paul.

A601 LKR, one of the last Transcontinentals built, is the first example operated by Translink. New to Indesit, it's

on a third engine but the original clutch remains. The lorry was sold by KT Trucks, Dartford, Kent, who are said to have discovered that if you tilt the cab on a slope the whole unit upends!

This unit has been all over Europe with Translink, and has even worked in Tunisia.

Final Transcon is Q393 OCR, new to the Ford Motor Company as a wrecker, without being road-registered. Bought in 1993, this lorry is normally used as a winch motor. This lorry boasts a most unusual Cummins engine. "It's obviously an

experimental engine - the torque curve and power band are definitely different to normal and we'd love to know more," Paul said.

Not surprisingly, the Fords have become famous locally. 'We have become known for them, and we sometimes get people ringing up asking if we have some sort of a widget for a Transcontinental," revealed Paul.

"They can attract a lot of attention. It's not unknown for us to pull up on a job and have people take photos or come up and say: 'They were a good truck in their day.'"

So, expect to see the Translink Transcons for a good while yet. "They're reliable, very well built and will go anywhere," said Paul, quipping: "Not only that, but they're definitely all paid for by now!"

Q393 OCR was new to the Ford Motor Company as a wrecker, and is believed to have an experimental Cummins engine.

Holmes 750 crane features a slogan of flat humour!